Teachings
from a
Classical Sufi Master

Teachings
from a
Classical Sufi Master

Extracts and abbreviations from
'Advice to the Seeker on the Path of Asceticism'
By
Sidi 'Ali al-Jamal

Selected and Translated By
Shaykh Fadhlalla Haeri

and

Shaykh Hosam Raouf

Zahra Publications

Distributed & Published by Zahra Publications
Centurion
South Africa

E-mail: info@shaykhfadhlallahaeri.com
info@zahrapublications.pub
© 2023 Shaykh Fadhlalla Haeri

Designed and typeset in South Africa by
Mizpah Marketing Concepts
Cover design by Margi Lake and Mariska Botes

The photograph of Shaykh Fadhlalla and Shaykh Hosam
on the back cover was taken by Ban Ebrahim

To purchase an eBook version of this book,
please visit www.zahrapublication.pub

For further information on Shaykh Fadhlalla Haeri and
his teaching please visit www.zahrapublications.pub
and www.shaykhfadhlallahaeri.com

ISBN No: 978-1-928329-43-5

Contents

Preface

One reads many books but only a few make an immediate and strong impression. These are books of transformation in which the subject matter emanates as an effulgence of light from the heart of the author, reflecting Reality and Truth. The words penetrate the hearts of the readers leaving them feeling as though the words were already in their hearts but only needed a bit of dusting to be revealed. When this takes place, joy overwhelms the readers and the book becomes a part of them. This book of Sidi 'Ali al-Jamal is one of these very rare books.

This rendering evolved out of a number of sessions during which Shaykh Fadhlalla dictated the extracts and abridgements, adding many explanations. Gratitude and thanks are due to all who assisted in its production, especially Najmah Ansari, Muna and Abbas Bilgrami, Mariska Botes, Ban and Haroun Ebrahim, Aliyah Batul Haeri, Muhammad Hussein Haeri, Muneera Haeri, Margi Lake, Muhammad Nanabhay, Ayesha and Abdul Karim Powell, Daliah Raouf, Alison Raouf, Safiyyah Surtee, Professor Sa'diyya Shaikh and Ahmed Baasith Sheriff.

I thank Allah and my brother, Shaykh Fadhlalla for the honour and privilege of being involved in producing this blessed book.

Shaykh Hosam Raouf

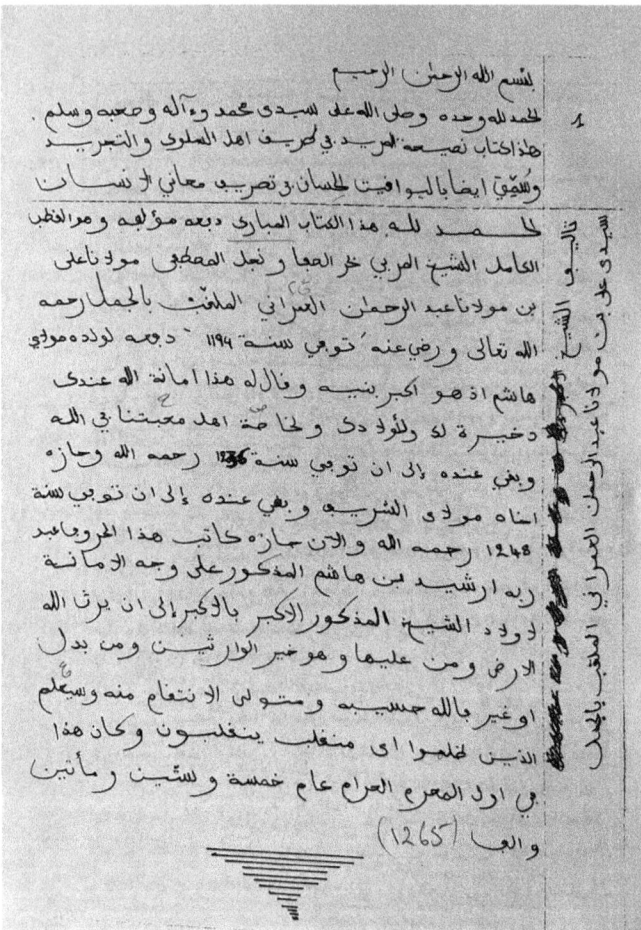

"Image of the first page of the handwritten copy
of the original manuscript used by
Shaykh Fadhlalla Haeri and Shaykh Hosam Raouf."

Introduction

The author of this book is the great Shadhili Shaykh Sidi 'Ali al-Jamal of Fez, Morocco, who died in 1194 Hijrah. The original Arabic title of the book was 'Advice to the Seeker on the Path of Asceticism' or 'Beautiful Rubies in Understanding the Meaning of Man'.

My first exposure to this book came through Diwan Press, 1977 complete translation of the text by Aisha 'Abd ar-Rahman at-Tarjumana, which was produced under the direction of Shaykh Abdulqadir al-Murabit. I loved the book, benefited from it, and was inspired to read the original in Arabic.

A photocopy of a handwritten version of the book later came into my possession. The original handwritten manuscript uses classical and Qur'anic Arabic and Sufi terminology with a Maghrebi vernacular. The style of the writing is free-flowing and repetitive, with long paragraphs and sentences covering several ideas in a charmingly quaint fashion. A method of exposition which was common practice with the learned men of past centuries, when books and reading were rare. This version was likely to have been handed down through several generations of the family of Ibn Ajiba (another great Moroccan Shaykh, who died in 1224 Hijrah). The manuscript was written in 1265 Hijrah in a partly colloquial Maghrebi script by the grandson of the author, with many variations in the quality of the writing, the size of the words and lengths of the sentences.

A few years on having enjoyed the book in the original Arabic, I felt inspired to produce a revised version with the topics rearranged, which would be more reader-friendly. By Allah's generosity, some of my close brothers and students in Islam, especially Shaykh Hosam Raouf, encouraged me to abridge, edit, and translate the book. Throughout this project, I felt the guiding light of the deceased author and his acceptance of this work.

Sidi Mustafa al-Basir, a contemporary Darqawi Shaykh, (died 1427 AH/2006 CE), told me that Sidi 'Ali al-Jamal had written a few pages at a time and dropped them from the window into the courtyard of his house. It was his successor, Moulay al-Arabi al-Darqawi, who collected the pages and put them together in the form of a book. When Sidi Mustafa visited us from Morocco in December 2002, he was delighted to hear this selection from Sidi 'Ali al-Jamal's work had just been completed. He, himself, had thought of doing something similar but had never managed it.

This rendering from Sidi 'Ali's work has been produced with the express purpose of serving the cause of original Islam and the Prophetic Household, from whom this Shaykh is descended.

Our ultimate accountability and gratitude is to Almighty Allah and His generosity.

Shaykh Fadhlalla Haeri

Explanatory Note to The Reader

We have tried to modernise some of the language but did not want to change concepts and ideas that were the norm at the time of Sidi 'Ali al-Jamal, even when they would not be used today.

Readers are advised to first read the text through, then to read over what makes sense to them and, finally, to try to see the interconnected text as a whole.

This book addresses seekers at different levels of spiritual development. It is a treatise on the life-long journey towards man's full potential.

The original text was in Maghrebi Arabic using Sufi terminology. Some of the terms used denote different meanings, the word 'annihilation' being an important example. It means the disappearance from the world of duality and separation, through total surrender, to the unique world of unity and gatheredness. This annihilation implies enlightenment through transcendence to pure consciousness from the realm of the discernible senses.

Other terms, such as 'gnostic', are used interchangeably with 'enlightened', '*arif*', a teaching shaykh, or a master. When the word 'inward' or 'inner' is used on its own, it means inwardly hidden, and 'outward' or 'outer' means outwardly manifest.

Some Sufi terms used here do not have an appropriate equivalent in English; hence a glossary of Arabic Sufi terms is included at the end of the book.

Preliminaries

Haqiqa[1] and *Shari'a*[2]

Shari'a is the beginning of all things and *Haqiqa* is the end of all things. When the beginning is great, all is great.

He who enters *Haqiqa* is like someone entering a vast desert. He must either be familiar with the large open expanse or he must be rescued from it. One should enter the desert only with a guide.

When the seeker joins *Haqiqa* and *Shari'a*, his knowledge of Allah's ways becomes perfect.

Shari'a without *Haqiqa* will destroy the seeker inwardly every time. *Haqiqa* without *Shari'a* destroys the seeker outwardly. A balance between *Haqiqa* and *Shari'a* is the attribute of the messengers, prophets, martyrs, and *awliya'* (friends of Allah – sing. *wali*).

Many ancient communities were destroyed because they were attached to *Shari'a* alone without having *Haqiqa*.

Shari'a is life for the body and *Haqiqa* is life for the *ruh* (the spirit/soul).

Whoever follows *Shari'a* without *Haqiqa* has gone astray, and whoever follows *Haqiqa* without *Shari'a* is an apostate. Whoever joins *Haqiqa* and *Shari'a* is successful.

---

1   Inner, ultimate reality, truth, science of the inner. From *'haqqa'*, to be true, right, just, authentic, valid, and *'haqqaqa'*, to realise, make something come true. The Divine Name, *al-Haqq*, the Truth, He whose being ·never changes.

2   Literally means the path, the main road. *Shari'a* is the riverside from where one takes water, the outer laws and boundaries. It is the code of conduct, behaviour, modality of a people based on the divine revelation of their prophet.

Haqiqa is hidden and is gatheredness. *Shari'a* is manifest and is separation. Wherever *Haqiqa* appears inwardly in action, it leads to different outer levels of appropriate separation.

The people of *Haqiqa* are indeed the people of the inward and of inner discipline.

He who wants to be in *Haqiqa* must elevate his people and stay within *Shari'a*. Thus, whoever is not a servant of *Shari'a* has no share of *Haqiqa*.

Shari'a is outer expression and *Haqiqa* is inner reality. *Shari'a* is separation and *Haqiqa* is gatheredness. Separation is the source of gatheredness and gatheredness is the source of separation.

Shari'a relates to habits and norms and the seekers desire change and the breaking of norms.

Know that *Shari'a* is a banner raised during a battle, and *Haqiqa* is the army. As long as the banner is upheld, the army is winning. When the banner falls, the army is defeated.

The *din* (life transaction between Allah and man, religion) continues and endures by the *Shari'a*. It is our capital, whereas *Haqiqa* is our profit and bonus.

The master of *Haqiqa* is rejected by all creation, except for the very few. Prophet Musa (Pbuh) (Moses) could not interpret or understand the actions of Khidhr (the servant of Allah with divinely inspired knowledge) who had more knowledge than he did, thus he objected to his actions. What chance then is there for the common people?

Prayer is of two types. The first is a sensory prayer of *Shari'a*, which is the prayer of the common people. The second is the real prayer of meaning, which is the prayer of the elite.[3] Whoever enters the prayer of meaning will not leave it as, it is said, "When the heart prostrates, it never rises."

All that is wisdom by choice is *Shari'a*, and all that is power by force is *Haqiqa*. You plant by *Shari'a* and reap by *Haqiqa*. You plant humility and reap might, and the reverse is true. Allah has created the action and ascribed it to you, and your action will enable you to seek Allah. Allah puts the option of planting good or evil in your hands, so that it will be a proof for you or against you.

Shari'a and *Haqiqa* are bound by gatheredness and released by separation. When *Haqiqa* binds, *Shari'a* releases and the opposite is true. All increase in existence is between binding and releasing. When *Haqiqa* is revealed *Shari'a* veils it and the opposite is true. When one exalts one debases and the reverse is true.

Haqiqa is inner beauty and gatheredness and outer majesty and separation. *Shari'a* is outer beauty and gatheredness and inner majesty and separation. The common people set out for *Shari'a* and neglect *Haqiqa*. The elite set out for *Haqiqa* and neglect *Shari'a*. The elite of the elite set out for Allah and reject all falsehood.

Whoever follows *Haqiqa* without *Shari'a* is like one who builds the foundation of a house but not the house itself, whereas the one who follows *Shari'a* without *Haqiqa* is like one who builds a house without a foundation.

Some people are veiled by *Shari'a* from *Haqiqa*, while some are veiled by *Haqiqa* from *Shari'a*. Whoever makes *Shari'a* the

---

3   The wise and mature seekers who have attained a high state of spiritual wisdom

door to *Haqiqa* is on the side of Allah. Allah says, "Enter houses through their doors." Whoever comes to the door of *Haqiqa* other than through the door of *Shari'a* will be turned away.

The master of *Haqiqa* is truly an *'arif* (gnostic) of Allah and is transformed by contemplation of Allah. Masters of *Shari'a* act by creation and are the disciplined people of this world.

Shari'a is slavery and *Haqiqa* is freedom. These two states alternate in man like day and night. He who recognises Allah in the bitterness of slavery will also recognise Allah in the sweetness of freedom. The real servant of Allah loses awareness of the bitterness and freedom and what follows belongs to Allah. The servant of states is destroyed in the states. The state of freedom is destroyed by its sweetness, and the state of slavery is destroyed by its bitterness. Allah says, "O world! serve whoever serves me, and exhaust whoever serves you."

You must understand that the people of *Shari'a* deny the people of *Haqiqa* and they are right to do this. However, if the people of *Haqiqa* deny the people of *Shari'a*, they are wrong. It is because the people of *Shari'a* are guards to the King and the role of the guards is to refuse entry to the King.

The people of *Haqiqa*, however, are they whose rejection by the people of *Shari'a* is not important to them. Therefore, they pardon all people including those who reject them, for they are annihilated from what is other-than-Allah. They are completely absorbed in their contemplation of the Master. The people of *Haqiqa* are already sitting with the King and the people of *Shari'a* are at the door.

Shari'a is outer wisdom and the common people are overcome by witnessing it. The elite are dominated by witnessing power and are inclined to it.

Power and wisdom are Allah's attributes.[4] The attribute of wisdom is always static, while the attribute of power is ever fresh. Power means turning to the unseen and to Allah without self-concern.

Shari'a was brought into existence as an indication of *Haqiqa*. Every *Shari'a* has a reality but not every reality is a *Shari'a*. Whoever enters the door of *Shari'a* reaches *Haqiqa*, whereas the reverse is not always true.

Annihilation in one's blessings is annihilation itself, whereas annihilation in the Blessor is the source of success. He who is annihilated in that with which he is blessed is miserable and he who is annihilated in Allah is perfect. Some of the things that stop one from reaching that state are existential pleasures and regrets.

People of *Haqiqa* are exiled and rejected, and the people of *Shari'a* are present and accepted. People of *Haqiqa* are attached to their Master and do not recognise other-than-Him. They are distracted from being occupied with this world, and Allah says, "Few are they" (the people of *Haqiqa*). All the mosques and gatherings and governments are only set up for *Shari'a* and its people. As for the people of *Haqiqa*, they have been given something by Allah that the common people do not have. The enlightened ones say, "I left the people, their *din* and their wealth, and sought You, O Allah! You are my *din* and my wealth."

---

4   Wisdom is to do with balance, whereas Power is pure energy. Wisdom relates to context and appropriateness, whereas Power is at all times. If Power is used appropriately it has entered the realm of Wisdom

Only *Haqiqa* can bear *Haqiqa*.

The one of *Haqiqa* has withdrawn from creation by contemplating the Real and has withdrawn from his annihilation in the means by contemplation of the Maker of means. His intoxication has overcome his sobriety and his gatheredness has overcome his separation. The perfect servant is he who drinks, and his sobriety is increased, and he who withdraws, and this increases him in presence. His gatheredness does not veil him from his separation, and his separation does not veil him from his gatheredness. His transformation does not bar him from his ongoingness and the reverse is true. He gives everything its due.

Some of the *fuqara'* (pl. *faqir*) repeatedly asked their Shaykh to guide them to the *Haqiqa* of wisdom. Their Shaykh asked them to come the following day, and when they arrived, he came out carrying a child in his arms and said, "Look at this child of mine. It has *'irfan* (enlightenment, gnosis), which you are seeking from me." At that moment, many doors opened for some of the students who understood those words, while the rest increased in bewilderment.

Existence and its Pattern

Existence is always full, never empty. It is full of either form or meaning. Whatever increases the form, decreases the meaning, and vice versa.

When you fear existence and existence overpowers you, your fear is a basic one. You can overcome your fear of existence by Allah. If, however, you rely upon yourself everything will overpower you and you will continue to fear everything.

Whenever the perfection of existence appears to an enlightened man it appears as something that is the perfection of the manifestation of power.

Whenever existence appears, non-existence appears after it and it is like that when non-existence appears—existence appears. Only the one who is beloved perceives the relationship of existence and non-existence and has the perfect courtesy, which comes through contemplation.

When you humble yourself to existence and give it power over you, existence humbles itself to you. The kingdom[5] of man resides in their service and their service is found within their leadership.

Allah made man a copy of existence and existence a copy of man, from the highest to the lowest. Man contains the highest things, the noblest things, as well as the smallest and most despicable.[6]

Your inner supports the outer aspects of existence and your outer supports the inner aspects of existence. Existence is like

---

5   Kingdom in this context indicates the realm of the human body, mind and heart, and all that governs wellness and illness

6   Whatever of existence that may be connected with or realised by human beings has its roots and essence in the human soul. It is seen in the outer but has its roots in the inner.

a tree and you are its roots, existence is like your body and you are its heart.

Know that the details of every created thing down to the smallest ant are recorded in existence. All of existence lies between gatheredness and separation and thus contains every gatheredness and every separation.

Know that all of creation is like the earth from which it has come. The earth in which you plant is the one from which you harvest.

Existence confronts you with perfection when your inner self reflects perfection and existence confronts you with imperfection when your inner self is imperfect. The Shaykh's advice to the *faqir* is, "Acknowledge your stupidity and ignorance, for this leads to intelligence and knowledge."

The Shaykh advised the *murid* (pupil), "Do not deny or ignore yourself when you have the urge to do something, for the self is like a trained dog - it only barks at the living. When the self is veiled it must be suspect, and when it is suspect it cannot be purified and made to grow" (i.e. do not keep hidden what is negative within you or it cannot be treated).

Allah has created existence for the sake of man as a mark of his honour and has created the human body as a mark of honour for the *ruh*. When the *ruh* departs, the body dies and if man departs, this existence will cease to exist.

Know that all existence flows according to the rules and the will of Allah. Part of the will of Allah is the will of His servant.

Know that existence and people are like mirrors. If you confront them with seriousness, they confront you in kind, and the same is true for beauty, majesty, separation, and gatheredness.

Existence can only be entered by the door of the self and the self is only entered by the door of existence.

Existence is from you and you are from it. According to the degree that you are its servant, it is your servant. According to the degree that you are its master, it is your master. According to how much you thank it, it thanks you. Similarly, if you debase and criticise it, it debases and criticises you. According to your truthfulness to it, it is truthful to you. According to your rejection of it, it rejects you. According to your wrongdoing, wrongdoing comes to you. According to your aversion to it, it is adverse to you. It is as if everything is in your hand.

Man is a copy of existence and existence is a copy of man. Man rules existence and existence is under the ownership of the human being. The kingdom of man is based on the kingdom of existence. What man wills is in existence but what existence wills in not in man. Man uses existence as the heart uses man. The heart is the house of Allah in man and the heart is in Allah's hand. Allah turns it according to divine Will.

Tariqa - The Path

This path of ours is prophetic and is based on *zuhud* (doing without). *Zuhud* is the way of transformation.

The path (*tariqa*) has three conditions: the first is the constant companionship of its people and its master, the second is to listen to them and behave accordingly, and the third is to be intimate with the people of *tariqa* and to behave like them.

The traveller on this path of ours relies on the highest thing outwardly, and that is friendship to the people of the Path. However, he is also a friend of the people of the lowest things. The people of *Haqiqa* respect and exalt the traveller, and the people of *Shari'a* shun and humiliate him.

The goodness of this path is in humbling the self and disregarding one's wealth. Departure from the path results in misery of the self and the illusion of profit. Allah says, "He buys from the *mu'mins* (believers) their selves and their property, and for that they have the Garden. The traveller on this path goes through three stages. The first is the outer stage of the common people, the second is the inner stage of the elite, and third is the outer stage of the elite of the elite.

The seeker of this path will only succeed if he is brave, resolute, and does not care about profit or loss. As for the fearful and cautious, there is no place for them on this path.

There are two paths to Allah and one leads to the other. The first is to do with nearness and the other with distance. The path of distance is the path of norms, and the path of nearness (to Allah) is the path of breaking norms.

This path of ours is called the path of the inner realm, which is the real realm. The outer realm is a copy of it and its shadow.

The first stage of this path occurs when the doors of the outer are blocked to the seeker, so that his Master comes to him. It is only after that that the doors of the unseen begin to open. The sun only rises after the darkness of the night.

It is said that great affliction and constriction are like festival days for those who know.

As for the *murid*, there is no day better for him than the day in which his inner and outer needs are great. At such times, the sincere *murid* must welcome his needs and not flee from them.

How can *Haqiqa* appear to you if you are occupied with self-concern and choice? How can your journeying be sound if you have desire, love, and hate? How can you attain a high rank, if your heart contains love of this world? How can your Lord be pleased with you, if you have not become thoroughly discontent with yourself? How will barriers fall for you, if you are only seeking pleasure? How can you be free, if you claim love for the Creator but really love His creation? Had you returned to His door, you would have found Him forgiving those who turn to Him in *tawba* (repentance, turning away from wrong actions).

A Shaykh had a young *murid* with him. The *murid's* parents forbade him from visiting his Shaykh. The Shaykh's advice to him was, "Obey your parents in everything, except in their telling you not to come here. Come to us, even if they disapprove."

The first thing that the self deals with is creation, then withdrawal from creation, then hunger, then travelling, then talking to ordinary people and to distinguished ones, then serving without asking for a wage, then wearing rough and basic clothes. These things are doors to Allah.

What is desired of the seeker is that he leaves the means. Once you leave the means, you will see the original cause of all means. When the servant is with servants, he wears the same garments, and when he is with his Lord, he wears the garment of sovereignty.

This path is the reverse of what the intellect understands and is thus beyond the understanding of the ordinary people. It is to do with divestment. Planting the impossible will only yield the impossible and planting norms only yields norms, for one plucks the fruits of that which one plants.

This path of ours is the path of essence and is described by the attributes of the Prophet (S), who was outwardly majestic and inwardly beautiful.

The Garden is surrounded by hateful things, whereas the fire is surrounded by attractive things.

The seeker of this path is like a corpse because a corpse does not speak, does not move, is not concerned with the self, does not organise or manage, does not resist good or evil and does not turn. Whoever speaks to him elicits no response.

Enlightened Beings (*Wali/'arif*)

The Shaykh said the reality of *wilaya* is that if you are sitting in the shade of the tent, you do not desire the sun, and if you are sitting in the sun you do not desire the shade. The man of Allah is he who sees by descent as well as by ascent. It is he who serves by retreating as well as by advancing. My Shaykh said, "If you are in the light and the people of darkness want to harm you, they will not be able to do it. Darkness does not reach light and their harm will return to them."

If the *'arif* scrutinises and examines the self, he will not find the weight of a mustard seed that is not correct. The *'arif* will find it perfect in every way. If you scrutinise the whole of existence, you will come to the same conclusion; it is always the perfection of perfection.

The self is a copy of existence and existence is a copy of the self. This knowledge is only obtainable from the company of the *'arifs*, if they can be found. They are the ones who do not reject any aspects of the self or of creation.

The Shaykh says, "I did not find a lover in existence equal to my soul. It is the most beloved of lovers to me. It is the spring of all good things and it is the spring of the secret of lights. I found nothing in existence, except good, and I did not concentrate on anything or turn to it, but I found it before me sooner than in the blink of an eye. My cure is in it and my healing is from it. My beginning is from it and my end is in it, it is my drink and it is my watering place. I seek it and it is my goal. My transformation is from it and my transformation is in it, my presence is in it and my intoxication is by it."

Foundations

The *Murid* and the Shaykh

Unless asked by the Shaykh, the *murid* should not eat with him, sleep near him, laugh in front of him and should not talk in an assembly without his permission. It is said: "Make your action salt (scarce) and your courtesy flour (abundant)."

Action is form and *adab* (appropriate conduct) is meaning. The seeker is the one who takes meaning as his asset.

The situation of the *murid* with the Shaykh is like that of the egg with the hen. The egg will only hatch after the hen incubates it; and without incubation, the egg will not develop. The *murid* should stay near to the Shaykh until the Shaykh departs.

The worst behaviour of the *murid* with his Shaykh is to talk much or make assertions. This is because speech is might and the *murid* is not yet in that state.

At the start of the journey, the relationship is the same as that of a mother and her child but at the end of the journey there may come a time when separation and weaning are necessary, especially in the outer relationship. The inner relationship between the serious *murid* and his Shaykh continues, since the everlasting connection is through the light of the ever-present connector, Allah, and true love continues.

To be a true servant of Allah, you must first be a true servant of someone who is the servant of Allah. If you want to achieve sincerity with Allah, be sincere with one who is truly sincere with Allah. If you want to be humble with Allah, then be humble with the shaykh, for he knows and practises humility before Allah. If you want to be joyful with Allah, be joyful with the servants of Allah. If you want to be thankful to Allah, then thank the servants who are truly thanking Allah.

If your *adab* is bad with a servant of Allah, then your *adab* towards Allah is bad. When you despise and have no respect for the servants of Allah, you have despised Allah, and when you consider yourself higher than the servants of Allah, you have placed yourself higher than Allah.

Whoever enters *Shari'a* without *Haqiqa* is sure to leave it. Perfection lies in entering *Haqiqa* by *Shari'a* at the hand of an accomplished teacher. Whoever enters *Haqiqa* at the hand of a shaykh, has entered *Haqiqa* by *Shari'a*.

Majesty is like a coarse garment. Beauty is like a garment of silk. The shaykh's duty is to make the wearing of coarse garments attractive to *murids* and to encourage them to avoid garments of beauty. For the *murid*, majesty and coarseness of garments are appropriate to his station. It is said that to witness beauty before having acquired the *adab* of majesty is to be rejected as a *dajjal* (deceiver, imposter). When the *murids* become men of intellect and can distinguish between things and their opposites, they will be ready for different robes.

Part of the *adab* of the *murid* with his Shaykh is that when the Shaykh tells him to go through the eye of the needle he does not turn away or hesitate.

If an enlightened *murid* says to his Shaykh, "If a creature harms me or causes my tears to flow, Allah will destroy it without delay." The Shaykh will say, "Allah has made me the opposite. I am patient with whoever injures me, and I laugh if I am harmed. Allah destroys he who harms me instantly."

When the *murid* meets his Shaykh, he is like a child finding his mother. The proximity of the child provokes milk in the mother's breast. When the *murid* sits before his Shaykh knowledge comes from the Shaykh.

The Shaykh needs the *murid* as the *murid* needs the Shaykh, for sometimes the Shaykh drinks from the vessel of the *murid* if that *murid's* inner eye is illuminated.

The *murid* is in great danger if he does not obtain the station of *rijal* (spiritual maturity) and receives knowledge and wisdom. Until he attains this state, he is in danger of being consumed by existence.

The successful *murid* is he who is transformed by his Master, has disappeared from himself and is other than himself. The key to his transformation is his annihilation in the *awliya'* of Allah. Whoever has no transformation by the *awliya'* of Allah has no transformation by Allah.

Whoever looks at the one who sees Allah will see Allah. The one who sees the one who sees Allah is like the one who sees Allah. Both are people of the same way, even though each has his own rank.

When the Shaykh of a *murid* dies, the *murid* is like the one who travels without a guide and must find another guide. Those who say the dead Shaykh is enough are ignorant and have little knowledge.

The seeker should not always be silent before the Shaykh. He who is (constantly) shy will not learn. If the *murid* does not speak, he is like a child with his parents; they will not know what is wrong with him and will not be able to prescribe the correct cure for his ailment.

A man came to a Shaykh and asked him, "I desire from Allah and you to direct me to a Shaykh who is perfect." The Shaykh answered, "My son, whoever has a perfect *murid*, he is your perfect Shaykh."

The perfect Shaykh is the one who directs you for the good of your self and saves you from its evils, until your (lower) self obeys you and avoids prohibitions. Then he takes you with kindness through the three stages of the people: being ordinary, being the elite, and being the elite of the elite, so that you do not see other than Him in existence.

The *karama* (miracle) appears to the *wali* in two aspects, one by overflowing joy and the other by guiding the *murids*.

The sincere *murid* is diligent in *dhikr* (remembrance of Allah, invocation) and his sincerity shows, because when man loves something, he repeatedly mentions it and when *dhikr* of Allah is continually on the tongue, wisdom flows.

A seeker who is content with the self or with the intellect is like one who travels in a dangerous land without a companion.

The hungry seeker is like a young and tender tree with a slender stalk. It only needs a small amount of water and nourishment. This seeker will take what is given to him by his Shaykh and grow accordingly. The old and established tree is content with what it has, like a self-opinionated old man who cannot learn.

The young seeker is like a clay vessel before it is baked in the fire. It is pliable and easy to knead and turn on the wheel.

The old seeker is like a vessel that has already been baked in the fire. It cannot accept more treatment even after it has been crushed in a mortar.

The *murid* at the beginning finds that creation rejects him and causes those who are near to flee from him. These are part of his trials; for the garden is surrounded by hated things and the *faqir* will only reap the fruits of knowledge when *Shari'a* and *Haqiqa* are one for him.

For he who keeps the company of an *'arif* of Allah and is sincere, it is the same whether his Shaykh is present or absent, he will benefit in the Shaykh's presence or absence. He will benefit from him when he is silent or when he speaks. In addition, if the veil between the *murid* and Allah has been lifted, he will benefit when the Shaykh dies as he benefited from him in his life.

The Shaykh says, "Beware of neglecting acknowledgement of the one who shows you openings, because to ennoble such a being brings about blessings and an increase in openings and help."

Once I complained to the Shaykh that my inner was correct, but my outer was not. He commanded me to imitate simplicity until I was described by it. When I planted simplicity in the inner, it bore me the fruit of intellect in the outer. Things can only be achieved by liking the opposite. When you are concerned with something inwardly, existence will confront you with the same, whether it is good or evil. Allah says: "I am in My servants' good opinion of Me."

Whoever aims for his Master and is sincere in his quest, even if he seeks him in stone, will find Him.

Knowledge and Actions

Knowledge is action and action is knowledge

Knowledge is in the position of the *ruh* and action is in the position of the body. One cannot exist without the other.

Sadness is the state of the person who does not combine the gift of knowledge with the gift of ignorance, or the gift of action with the gift of inaction. It is this balanced condition that leads to real happiness. It is said that the *'arif* prays that his ultimate destination in love is to be coloured by experiencing change and the opposites.

When knowledge accompanies action, its virtues are great. There are people of knowledge who do not act and others who act with no knowledge. They are ignorant. Those who have a lot of knowledge and act accordingly are accomplished. Indeed, action based on knowledge will lead to more knowledge.

The Prophet of Allah (S) has said, "Whoever acts by what he knows, Allah will give him knowledge of that which he did not know."

The moment of knowledge is not the same as the moment of action. That is because Allah "has not placed two hearts in a man's breast." Man is looking at either beauty or majesty, but not at the two at the same time.

Know that it is impossible for knowledge to exist without action. Similarly, it is impossible for action to exist without knowledge.

There is no hierarchy between knowledge and action, because sometimes authority belongs to knowledge and action follows from it and sometimes the reverse is true.

The master of the outer, plants his orchard with *Haqiqa* and it bears fruit in creation. The master of the inner, plants his orchard in existence and it bears fruit with Allah. The master of the outer, plants his orchard with gatheredness of himself, and it bears him the fruit of separation in existence. The master of the inner, plants it by separation in existence and it bears him the fruit of gatheredness in himself. What a difference between the one who plants separation and harvests the fruit of gatheredness and the one who plants gatheredness and harvests the fruit of separation!

Knowledge is light, and action is darkness. When action dominates knowledge, it is the state of striving. When knowledge dominates action, it is the state of contemplation.

The Shaykh's advice is, "Make your action scarce and your knowledge abundant."

Essence and Attributes

Allah manifests Himself to His servants either in Essence or in Attributes

All existence has essence and attributes in it. Essence is the source of all attributes and attributes the source of essence. Attributes conceal themselves when essence appears and vice versa. Whoever turns to you with attributes, confront him with essence and you will overcome him, and the reverse is true.

There are two gardens: the Garden of Essence and the Garden of Attributes. The Garden of Essence is the Garden of Witnessing and Realisation and the Garden of Attributes is that of beauty and ardent love. The Garden of Essence is the Garden of Transformation by Attributes and ongoingness by Essence, and the Garden of Attributes is the Garden of Transformation by Essence and ongoingness by Allah.

Silence, blindness, deafness, abasement and stupidity are essence, and speech, seeing, hearing, might, and intelligence are attributes.

Allah's power is gatheredness and His wisdom is separation. Allah bestows the attributes of power and wisdom on those of His servants whom He favours. These attributes alternate one or the other upon him like day and night, summer and winter.

The attribute of power concerns might, strength, hope, expansion, beauty, giving, nearness, etc. The instances in which wisdom manifests include: incapacity, poverty, abasement, weakness, fear, contraction, majesty, withholding, distance, etc.

Silence and Speech

Speech is high, and silence is low.

Silence can be higher and nobler than speech, if based on knowledge. Speech can be lower than silence, if based on ignorance.

When man speaks, his speech limits him, yet when he is silent the possibilities are limitless.

The one who is silent and knowledgeable possesses all existence, high and low, for he acts on Allah's command.

It is said that silence due to ignorance is better than speaking with ignorance, whereas speaking from knowledge is nobler than keeping silent out of ignorance.

The one who is silent from knowledge is like a lion outwardly and inwardly, whereas the one who speaks with ignorance is like a hyena outwardly and inwardly.

When the person of silence meets with the one who speaks, the silent one prevails over the one who speaks and not the other way around. Silence is low whereas speech is high, and whatever is low prevails in every case. Allah says in the Qur'an, "We want those who are humble in the land to be the inheritors."

The *'arif* who obtains the fruit of the meanings sees that silence makes speech pleasant and speech makes silence pleasant, for all things are only pleasant by their opposites.

Speech is beauty for creation and majesty for oneself. Silence is beauty for oneself and majesty for creation. Speech is separation for the self and silence is gatheredness for the self.

Whoever speaks is owned by his speech and whoever is owned is abased. Whoever is silent owns and is exalted. He who speaks by Allah is the one for whom speech and silence are the same.

If the one of the outer is silent his silence is imperfect and if he speaks his speech is imperfect and it is the reverse for one of the inner. The one of the outer may maintain the appearance of perfection but his tongue will betray him. The one of the inner may appear imperfect but his tongue will defend him.

Outer and Inner

The people of outer knowledge do not give much importance to inner knowledge and the people of the inner do not give much importance to the people of the outer. The Qur'an says, "Every party rejoices in that which is theirs."

The perfect *'arif* gives everyone and everything its due and its appropriate portion. He looks at the people of the outer by their outwardness and at the people of the inner by their inwardness and thus has authority over all.

The *'arif* of Allah does not clash with the people of the outer, nor does he fall under their power. He always obtains goodness out of every state.

The people of the outer kingdom are not established in their kingdom until they are in harmony with the people of the inner and the reverse is true. This connection is fundamental and is from before time, for all kingdoms belong to Allah.

Outer knowledge and action reduce inner knowledge and action and vice versa. The place of profit is the place of loss. Either the heart is filled with the outer or it is filled with the inner.

In the same way that actions diminish words, inner action will diminish outer action.

Wisdom relates to connecting the inner with the outer and whatever relates to the inner dominates the outer.

The perfect among the people of the inner, after acquiring the fruits of the inner take what is available from the outer, for they are considered amongst the men of Allah. The people of the inner flee from the people of the outer as though they are fleeing from a lion. They say that the inner is the heart of the present and the real, and the limbs of creation are the outer.

The heart of the being is like a king and all the outer extremities and inner organs are its emissaries. The inner is always the sultan and the ruler.

The outer involvement of the people of the path decreases as their inner knowledge increases, and the reverse is true for those who are not on the path.

People of outer knowledge and action have no entitlement to the secrets of the heart. The heart contains knowledge of the unseen world, but their portion is only in the outer.

If a person from the outer sincerely intends to seek the face of Allah, he will move from station to station by stages.

The nature of the inner is like that of sleep. He who has experienced it cannot fully define it in words.

The *adab* of the people of the outer relates to creation, and the *adab* of the people of the inner relates to *Haqiqa*. The principle is the same, but one group belongs to Allah and the other to creation.

That which belongs to Allah becomes gathered and that which belongs to creation becomes dispersed.

Whoever gathers his inner must separate from his outer and vice versa. The good in gatheredness is in the servant's keeping company with himself, and this can only be found by being close to a master of the path.

Part of the state of the one of the outer is that ignorance accompanies him because darkness dominates him. Part of the quality of the one of the inner is that because light dominates him knowledge does not leave him. Darkness is like a tree whose fruit is ignorance and whose condition is denial. Light is like a tree whose fruit is knowledge and whose condition is submission and affirmation.

The leaders of the inner are the *awliya'* and the *'arifs* of Allah. The leaders of the outer are the kings and their followers.

When one of the kings of the outer and one of the kings of the inner meet, existence comes to their hands as through an open door. The kings of the outer are not established or confirmed except by harmony with the kings of the inner. Similarly, the masters of the inner are not established or confirmed except by harmony with the kings of the outer. The people of the outer are the people of separation, and the people of the inner are the people of gatheredness. Things only establish themselves by their opposites. People of the outer aim for the outer therefore they find the outer and the reverse is true. When the people of the outer find one of the people of the inner, they love him but cannot keep his company. Only the *'arifs* can understand this.

Dhikr is of two types: the inner *dhikr* of thought and the outer *dhikr* of speech. The people of outer *dhikr* speak it by their tongues and the people of inner *dhikr* express it in their hearts. Words veil the people of outer *dhikr* and the people of inner *dhikr* contemplate the essence.

The seen and the unseen beset man, like two wives competing over him, and whoever wins him boasts to the other wife.

Nothing in existence is more pleasant than the pleasures of nearness and of distance, and the pleasures of gatheredness and of separation. These meanings are the foundation of *'irfan.*

Outer action follows the norms and inner action is the breaking of norms.

If you want results, join your outer with your inner and your outer action with your inner action. The combination will have the attributes of knowledge and of action. Its essence is light, and its name is *khalifa* (successor, representative).

Obtain wisdom by connecting the inner with the outer. Whatever comes from the inner dominates the outer.

For the ordinary people, outer generosity brings about inner miserliness. For the people of heart, their outer meanness relates to their inner generosity.

Illumination of the outer results in gifts of action whereas illumination of the inner results in gifts of knowledge. When the outer is illuminated, the inner is and vice versa. People of *'irfan* do not rejoice in light nor do they grieve in darkness. Their joy is with the Creator of both light and darkness.

For the people of the inner, their realm has a hundred divisions; ninety-nine belong to the unseen and one to the seen. For the people of the outer, their kingdom has a hundred divisions; ninety-nine belong to the seen and one to the unseen.

The Sensory World and the World of Meaning

Know that good that manifests in outer sensory action also has an inner meaning. The same is true for evil. Perfection lies in the manifestation of actions that connect the sensory world to the world of meaning.

The enlightened being accepts the results of good and evil actions in every case because he is with neither good actions nor evil actions. In all states he is with the Master.

The wise being connects the sensory world to the world of meaning and vice versa. He also connects the essence with the attributes and vice versa.

Whoever seeks meaning must subdue the sensory world, and whoever wants the sensory world must ignore the world of meaning. The sensory world is separation and the world of meaning is gatheredness.

The sensory world bases itself on meaning. In the sensory world, physicality has authority over meaning, although they are often connected. In the next world, meaning has authority over the physical.

Know that all harm occurs to you either at the sensory level or at the level of meaning. If treatment starts soon after harm occurs you will be restored, but the longer the condition remains untreated, the more difficult it will be to heal.

Whatever increases meaning causes decrease at the sensory level and the reverse is true. The seeker is an interspace between the two. Both the sensory world and the world of meaning are his servants. It is the reverse with the ignorant man. He is the servant of the sensory world and of the world of meaning and they compete with each other over him.

When the essence manifests, sensory things appear, and meanings withdraw. When attributes appear, meanings appear, and sensory things withdraw.

The end of the world of the senses is the beginning of the world of meaning and there is no end to the world of the senses or to the world of meaning. Thus, the seeker of the world of meaning is never fully satisfied and the same is true for the seeker of the sensory world.

Meanings are roots and sensory things are trees. Sensory things only exist by meaning, just as trees only exist by their roots.

The fire of the sensory level is kindled, and its flames are fanned when the wood that is its meaning is thrown in and the same is true for the fire of meaning, when its sensory wood is thrown in. The flames leap, blazing and burning, until the removal of the sensory wood from the fire.

Tawhid - Divine Presence

Divine presence is like a garden into which the one with envy cannot enter. Nor can anyone who has hate, rancour, anxiety, worry or any of the other veils of the lower self.

Know that *shirk* (associating power with other-than-Allah) is the foundation of all evil and the foundation of all good. To confuse them is to stray from the right path and is thus a perversion. Shaykh Abdul Qadir al-Jilani said, "Connect your gatheredness and sever your separation."

Allah is light, and this world is darkness and light does not mix with darkness. Whenever the heart fills with light, it overflows into the rest of the body and when it fills with darkness the darkness manifests in all parts of the body.

Allah, the Exalted, is One in His essence, attributes, and action. He is gathered so there is no separation in Him and is separated so there is no gatheredness in Him. In His gatheredness is proof of His separation, and in His separation is proof of His gatheredness.

If you recognise Allah in everything, nothing will enslave you, for Allah says, "Oh world, serve whoever serves Me and exhaust whoever serves you."

Allah is One and from Allah comes two, and from the two come four. The two are the outer and the inner and the four are the outer sensory world and the outer world of meaning, the inner sensory world and the inner world of meaning.

In total there are eight realities:

- Outer sensory earthly;
- Outer meaning earthly;
- Inner sensory earthly;
- Inner meaning earthly;
- Outer sensory heavenly;
- Outer meaning heavenly;
- Inner sensory heavenly;
- Inner meaning heavenly.

These eight realities oppose each other. Whenever something obsesses you, go to its opposite and it will be in order.

Creation and Creator

Whoever leaves the presence of his Master, will find that phenomenal things have power over him. They will take him, bind him, and constrict him. This is the repayment for his negligence in the presence of Allah. He has created you as His servant and has created phenomenal things as your servants. Whenever you neglect the service of your Master phenomenal things will overwhelm you. Either you witness the presence of your Creator, or you witness the presence of His creation.

Know that anyone who avoids creation will need it and must connect with it. Equally, anyone whom creation avoids will be needed by it, and must be connected with it, whether they like it or not. This is because all of existence has both gatheredness and separation in it.

He who turns to creation has turned away from the Creator, and he who flees from creation is turning to Allah.

Know that creation turns away from whoever seeks it and seeks whoever abandons it. Your Master always seeks you, therefore seek Him alone. Know that whoever seeks anything will not attain it, until he spends of himself and his wealth on it. What a loss that is, and what a profit! The one who spends himself in seeking the One, Allah will increase him in it many times over.

Faith

My Shaykh has instructed me regarding *iman* (faith, trust, belief, acceptance) saying, "Part of *iman* in the unseen is that your provision comes from where you do not expect, because the Prophet (S) said, 'Allah refuses to provide for His servant, the *mu'min*, except from whence he will not reckon'."

Prostration is of two kinds, one is to do with *Shari'a* and separation, and the other with *Haqiqa* and gatheredness. *Shari'a* and *Haqiqa* go together and whoever combines them is one who obeys the Messenger, and whoever obeys the Messenger, obeys Allah.

Man must be on guard against himself and against creation at all times. Goodness and evil will come equally from both him and from creation. The source of continuing good is Allah alone.

Fundamental Laws

The Opposites

By His Unique Oneness Allah created everything in pairs. Praise and blessings to Allah, Who gave everything its opposite, and each desires its opposite! Existence appears between the two opposites. When one opposite overcomes the other, it destroys the lesser.

Know that Allah has created everything with its opposite. All that is unknown is known by its opposite. Everything that is disunited is united by its opposite. All that is wrong is mended by its opposite. All that is right is ruined by its opposite. Everything has come into existence by connection of the opposites and returning to non-existence is by connection of the opposites. Life is between the connection of opposites, and death is by connection of the opposites. Nearness is only between the connection of the opposites, and so are distance, love, hate, might and abasement. His wisdom is in His power, and His power is in His wisdom. Glory be to the All-Knowing!

The key to earthliness is heavenliness, and the key to abasement is might. The key to *Haqiqa* is *Shari'a*, and vice versa. The key to death is life, and vice versa. The same applies to greatness and insignificance, arrival and departure, wideness and narrowness, gatheredness and separation, majesty and beauty. Thus, you find that the greatest of what is in existence relates to the most trivial, and the most immense relates to the smallest. Glory be to the Wise, All-Knowing, Whose judgement of the small things is as His judgement of the great things!

Inner illumination may appear outwardly dark in man, and thus creation flees from him. He who is outwardly luminous may possess little inner knowledge.

Immense light will only emanate from immense darkness, and immense vastness can only emerge from immense narrowness. Similarly, immense might can only come about from immense abasement. Nearness comes from distance, expansion from contraction, giving from withholding, profit from loss, and gatheredness from separation. Glory be to the One Who has made all things hidden with their root in their opposites!

Sensory things are of two types, as are the things of meaning, for Allah created everything in pairs when Allah brought existence into being and in existence human beings experience mercy, as well as punishment.

The people of outer beauty come to beauty by choice, and whoever is in such a state by choice, its opposite will come to him by necessity. Those who seek increase, decrease will come to them. The people of the inner turn to decrease and for them there is only increase.

The enlightened teacher leads his followers from the direction of imperfection and desire to perfection and contentment. Whoever looks at his own imperfection, perfection will come to him.

Allah has created man from existence as Allah created existence from him and it is because of this man's nature changes.

He who occupies himself with the Divine Names is veiled from the Essence, and he who occupies himself with the Essence will be veiled from the Names. The Names relate to the attributes. The Essence veils the attributes, and the attributes veil the Essence. *Shari'a* veils *Haqiqa*, and *Haqiqa* veils *Shari'a*, just as gatheredness veils separation, and separation veils gatheredness. The sensory world veils the world of meaning and the world of meaning veils the sensory world. Divine existence is based on its apparent absence, and this apparent absence is veiled by existence, just as Allah's nearness veils Allah's distance and vice versa. Understand, reflect and recognise that these are truly Allah's ways.

When you confront people with seriousness, they confront you with light heartedness and vice versa. The *'arifs* of Allah change constantly. The perfect *wali* (friend of Allah - plural *awliya'*) changes with all states and receives what he desires. People of this world constantly seek their own kind and the people of the next world constantly seek their kind.

The fundamental wisdom is that the key to all things lies in their opposites. If you desire great things, you must possess small things and vice versa. The highest thing finds the lowest thing and the lowest thing finds the highest thing. They are forever connected.

The key to heaven is earth and the key to might is abasement and vice versa. The key to *Haqiqa* is *Shari'a*, and the reverse is true. The key to corruption is righteousness, and the same is true with regard to nearness and distance, wealth and poverty, hunger and fullness, greatness and smallness, life and death, arrival and departure, wideness and narrowness, beauty and ugliness, gatheredness and separation. The key to perfect majesty is perfect beauty. All of existence travels from one opposite to another and is always moving in one direction or the other.

Whoever is humble towards existence by choice, existence is humble towards him by necessity, and whoever puts himself higher than existence by choice, existence emerges higher than him by necessity. Whatever you confront existence with, it confronts you with its opposite. Existence is a copy of you and you are a copy of it. Existence is in separation and you are its gatheredness. Existence is your essence and you are its attribute. It is your majesty and you are its beauty. It is your body and you are its *ruh*.

Know that in this existence Allah has created good and evil. Then Allah made a third kind from them and that is a mixture of good and evil. Creation is constantly occupied with sorting out this mixture and this will continue until the Day of Reckoning.

Know that Allah has made all things with form and with meaning. Their existence is hidden in their non-existence and their non-existence is hidden in their existence. Know that the cure for an illness is within the illness itself. Bistami was asked, "When is the illness of the self its remedy?" and he replied, "When the self opposes its passions, its illness is its remedy."

Things are only sought by their opposites. Beauty is sought by majesty and majesty is sought by beauty. The seeker of might is abased and the seeker of abasement is made mighty.

Know that he who persists in evil will eventually transform into good, for there must be change. Whoever wants to remain in one state will not succeed, for Allah's way as far as creation is concerned is constant change. There is a big difference between people upon whom change is imposed and people who accept change.

Whoever you exalt exalts you and whoever you abase abases you. However, both you and your money are exceptions to this rule, for whenever you exalt them, they abase you and whenever you abase them, they exalt you.

Whoever wants to overcome, is himself overcome, and whoever wants to be overcome, overcomes. Whoever wants to own is owned, and whoever wants to be owned, owns. Whoever wants to be exalted is abased, whoever wants to be abased is exalted.

As light has force (or power), so darkness has force. As strength has force, so too weakness has force. As power has force, incapacity has force. As speech has force, silence has force. As the highest in people has force, so does the lowest in people. When someone confronts you with anything and you confront him with its opposite, you will overcome him.

Gatheredness and Separation[7]

Gatheredness in the outer is separation in the inner, and separation in the outer is gatheredness in the inner. Gatheredness helps separation until separation becomes gatheredness. Gatheredness dominates separation in the inner, as separation dominates gatheredness in the outer. The *awliya'* are equal in gatheredness and separation and neither state is veiled. Separation is the source of gatheredness, and the reverse is true.

Separation is majesty and gatheredness is beauty. All that is beauty and gatheredness in your outer is all that is majesty and separation in your inner, and the reverse is true.

Whenever majestic separation takes over your outer, and beautiful gatheredness takes over your inner, the situation reverses itself, so that beautiful gatheredness takes over your outer and majestic separation takes over your inner.

Being put out and troubled is an attribute of separation and being at ease and trouble-free is an attribute of gatheredness. Whoever witnesses gatheredness is in expansion and whoever is dominated by separation experiences constriction.

You turn constantly from separation to gatheredness and vice versa.

Man is created between gatheredness and separation. Sometimes a person's gatheredness dominates his separation, and sometimes it is the reverse. When gatheredness dominates, knowledge dominates action and when separation dominates, action dominates knowledge. Allah says in the Qur'an, "Are those who know and those who do not know equal?"

---

7   Separation is an essential reality of the human condition, while gatheredness comes from Reality itself. Without gatherdness gnosis or *'irfan* is not possible, while without separation worship is not possible.

Gatheredness and separation alternate in every human being as summer follows winter. The elite recognise separation and they reach the kingdom of gatheredness. The ordinary people appear to be free until slavery due to separation comes to them.

If you want to have gatheredness, you must have words, and if you want to have separation, you must have action. The words of the inner are reflection and the words of the outer are *dhikr*. *Dhikr* is masculine reflection, meditation is feminine reflection, and gatheredness is their child.

The attribute of sovereignty is gatheredness and the attribute of slavery is separation. Whoever seeks separation from everything, including himself, must seek the attributes of freedom, and whoever wants to be gathered to everything must take on the attributes of slavery.

The attributes of freedom include: might, pride, power, wealth, strength, hearing, sight, speech, etc. All belong to gatheredness. Whoever takes on any of these attributes, his affairs will be in separation.

The attributes of slavery include: abasement, humility, incapacity, poverty, weakness, silence, lowering the eye, lack of hearing, etc. All belong to separation. Whoever shows any of these characteristics, his affairs will be in separation until they lead him to gatheredness and draw his heart to the presence of his Lord. This is the meaning of the statement "If you realise your attributes, He will help you with His attributes."

Sovereignty is gatheredness, and from gatheredness comes separation.

The inner gathers you to Allah and separates you from His creation. The outer gathers you to creation and separates you from Allah. Whoever recognises Allah outwardly and inwardly is enlightened.

The breaking of norms is separation, for norms are gatheredness. The breaking of norms is majesty in the outer and beauty in the inner. For the seeker, separation is in his outer and gatheredness is in his inner, because separation is darkness and gatheredness is light, and the place to witness Allah is in the enlightened heart.

The path to Allah of the *'arif* is such that the seeker should not look at separation but dive into the ocean of gatheredness. He will find that separation emanates from gatheredness.

Whoever claims gatheredness without separation claims the impossible, for this proclaims the invalidity of slavery. Whoever claims separation without gatheredness claims the invalidity of Allah's sovereignty. Whoever realises that separation is the source of gatheredness has realised perfection.

One recognises the value of gatheredness by separation and vice versa.

Knowledge is information about arrival and is separation. Action is arrival itself and is gatheredness.

Reflection is the noblest of all aspects of worship when it is gathered. When reflection separates, outer *'ibada* (worship, adoration) is more appropriate.

Beauty and Majesty

Our path is majesty outwardly and beauty inwardly, and whoever is on this path only abases himself to his Master. When the one on the path increases in outer majesty, he increases in inner beauty.

Know that beauty follows majesty, either by force or by choice. Everything in creation accompanies its opposites, knowingly or unknowingly.

When you offer majesty to people, they offer beauty in return, and the reverse is true. Opposites only attract their opposite, and this is the wisdom of Allah.

When confronted with majesty you should confront it equally with beauty, so that *Haqiqa* does not cut you off from creation.

The Master of majesty owns all existences and so does the Master of perfect beauty, because majesty emanates from beauty and vice versa.

If you want outer beauty, you must have inner beauty. Inner majesty forms outer majesty and vice versa.

All people are intoxicated. Their intoxication is by two means: the wine of beauty makes some drunk, while others are drunk with the wine of majesty. The wine of beauty is from elements of *arwah* (pl of *ruh*, soul), while the wine of majesty is from elements of form. All people are drunk by one or the other. These two wines are the basis for the Adamic human's existence. Without them, existence would vanish. The people who are intoxicated by the wine of beauty are kings, because their wine relates to Allah. The people who are drunk by the wine of majesty are servants.

Generosity is outwardly beautiful and inwardly majestic, and meanness is the opposite. Generosity is outwardly heavenly and inwardly earthly, and meanness is the opposite. The generous person is outwardly free and inwardly enslaved, and meanness is the opposite. The light of the generous person is in his outer and his darkness is in his inner. The darkness of a miser is in his outer and his light is in his inner.

Leaders and Leadership

Whoever places himself in a position of leadership will find he is truly a leader, and whoever places himself in the position of a servant will truly be a servant.

People of leadership are of four kinds, of which there are two outer kinds and two inner kinds. The first kind comprises of those who seek the pleasures of this world and it results in them being cut off from the inner. The members of the second kind seek results in this world and experience blessings from Allah. The third kind, which is the first of the inner, belongs to Allah and the results of its members belong to Allah, and they see His blessing. The fourth kind comprises those who are simply looking at the face of Allah at all times. They do not recognise anything except Him. The Master veils the first kind; He Who blesses veils the second kind; inner blessings veil the third group, and members of the fourth kind have no veil at all. Their Master's gatheredness occupies them. They only recognise Him, and He transforms them by His Essence, and their going-on is in Him.

The people of the outer are the people of separation and their strength is from the Names of Allah. The people of the inner are the people of gatheredness, and their strength lies in the contemplation of Allah. The people of the Names acquire the gifts of knowledge and action by the Names. The people of contemplation acquire the gifts of knowledge and action through their contemplation. The people of the Names are discriminated by their striving. The people of contemplation are discriminated by witnessing the moment. They are occupied by pleasant conversation, which protects them from all distractions. The station of the people of contemplation is clothed in a light, which penetrates all hearts emanating from them due to the Source of certainty. The one of the Names is always striving to cast off his veil. He acquires the gifts of gnosis. The one of contemplation is always witnessing the object of worship. He acquires the station of witnessing and the gifts of gnosis. Because of that, his rank is higher than others on the path.

Good and Evil

Wherever good is great, evil is great. Wherever benefit is great, loss is great. Wherever lovers come near, enemies come near, and wherever light is strong, darkness is strong.

It is the enlightened beings that truly see that each thing is hidden in its opposite, and that there is no separation. In this state, only absorption into the Source and the Ocean of Wonders remains. This is the goal of all seekers.

Know that the place of good is the place of evil, and that you are in an interspace between them. When you are angry, evil seeks you, and when you are with evil, good then seeks you. This is the law regarding both the outer and the inner. The Qur'an says, "If Allah knows of any good in your heart, He will give you better."

Whoever can use good can also use evil, and the reverse is true. For people who use much good and little evil, their goodness dominates their evil. For people who use much evil and little good, their evilness dominates their good.

When you are confronted with evil and you confront it with good, you will overcome the evil by your goodness because goodness is earthly, and evil is heavenly. The perfect *'arif* confronts evil either with greater evil or with goodness, which is stronger than evil. In this way, he overcomes evil at all times.

Know that what appears to some people as good does have benefit in it but that equally there is harm in it. Evil also has both benefit and harm in it, because the root of good and evil is the same. Allah says He will test you with both good and evil. He sometimes punishes by good and sometimes He brings down mercy by evil.

People of knowledge leave both good and evil and simply occupy themselves with the Creator of both. He is enough for them. Since they are His servants, both good and evil are their servants. The enlightened being benefits from both good and evil. While he occupies himself with his Creator, he is by Allah in good as well as in evil, and he recognises his Master in both. He is neither in good nor in evil, but is the same in both, for he is with the Master of both.

When the servant is with his Master, he increases and benefits from every state and no state harms him.

Know that when you do not do well to the people of this world, they will face you with evil.

As good only comes into existence by wisdom or power, so it is with evil. As they only come into existence by the door of wisdom or power, wisdom or power bring increase of existence both high and low. Heavenly increase relates to good, and earthly increase relates to evil. This is the case as far as the common people are concerned. As for the elite, either is good.

Do not let anyone bind you to good or evil, because man may be tied to the good of people in him or he may be tied by his good to people. He may also be tied by his evil to people, and he may be tied by the evil of people to him. The Shaykh said, "Evil comes to the house and knocks on the door. The man asks, 'Who are you?' Evil answers, 'I am evil'. The man says, 'Go away, I have no need of you'. Then evil sits by the door until good comes and knocks. When the man opens the door for it, good enters and evil sneaks in behind it. Had you not opened the door for good, evil would not have been able to enter."

Ibn Mashish says, "The seeker must turn to *tawba* (repentance, turning away from wrong actions) from his good and his evil, and he must turn to greater *tawba* for his good deeds than for his evil deeds. It is said, "The *tawbah* from the act of rebellion is one *tawba*, and the *tawba* from the act of obedience is a thousand *tawbas*."

Allah says in the Qur'an: "*Shaytan* (Satan, the Devil) is your enemy so take him as an enemy." The enemy desires to come between you and your Beloved. When you are preoccupied with his hostility, he achieves his desire, which is you missing your Beloved.

Shaytan is the Imam of the *kafirs* (deniers of Reality) and their model. When his Master appeared to him in gatheredness, he prostrated and when he appeared to him in separation by *Shari'a*, he denied Him. Allah informed *Shaytan* that there would be many others travelling in his footsteps. The *kafir* recognises Allah in gatheredness and in *Haqiqa* but rejects Him in separation and in *Shari'a*.

Part of His subtle mercy and generosity to you is His creation of *Shaytan* for you and your passions, so that He stirs you to His presence by heedlessness. Had it not been for His love for you, He would not have given *Shaytan* power over you.

Earthly and Heavenly

In reality, all actions are earthly, because they relate to the sensory world. Words are the reverse, because they come from the land of meaning.

An increase in existence occurs when the man of meaning meets the man of words. Then actions are heavenly, and words are earthly. The man of action dominates, as the root of action is high, and the root of words is low.

When the man of action is heavenly, and the man of words is earthly, the man of words dominates. When the man of action is earthly, and the man of words is heavenly, the man of action dominates. The earthly always dominates. When a man of words meets another man of words and their words are both earthly, the one whose sensory level is stronger dominates.

When the earthly quality is weak in respect to both the sensory world and the world of meaning and you want to strengthen it, you must descend to the earthly reality. It will then strengthen both the sensory world and the world of meaning. When an aspect is weak in the heavenly reality in respect to both the sensory world and the world of meaning and you want to strengthen it, you must then rise to the heavenly reality.

Behaviour of existence is of two divisions: earthly, which is inner and inspirational and heavenly, which is outer and physical. Earthly is with the self and *himma* (spiritual yearning) Heavenly is with the body and material.

Any decrease in this world increases heavenly behaviour.

Increase of action increases the rise of this world. Heavenly behaviour is the outer sultan, and the earthly behaviour is the inner sultan who has knowledge.

If the heavenly realm meets with the earthly realm and the meeting is for a good reason, then much good will come from it. Understand that the earthly has the upper hand. Equally, if the meeting is for evil, much evil will ensue, and both realms will be harmed. The earthly is still above and stronger than the heavenly.

When earthly things meet heavenly things, authority belongs to the earthly. The low always prevails over the high. When earthly speech meets heavenly speech, authority belongs to the earthly, not the heavenly. When heavenly actions meet earthly actions, authority belongs to the earthly. When words meet action, authority belongs to action.

Authority always belongs to earthly realities. They say that speech is silver, and silence is golden. Authenticity always belongs to the silent over the speaker. All earthly realities are *Shari'a* while heavenly realities are *Haqiqa*. Allah is both in the heavens and in the earth and He is the light of the heavens and the earth.

Each reality has heavenly and earthly aspects and corresponds to an aspect of the self and of existence. What is from the self is heavenly and what is from creation is earthly.

The eye has two realities: a heavenly reality, which is looking, and an earthly reality, which is lowering the eye. Just as the glance of the eye breaks the norms, so does lowering it. The wisdom of the glance of an eye is recognised by all people because it is heavenly, especially to the ordinary people. The wisdom of lowering the eye is only recognised by the elite, who dive into the knowledge of low and high things.

The Journey

The Seeker and the Wayfarer

The seeker is like the *hammam* (steam bath). When he is hot (gathered), he needs no attention, but when he is cold (in separation), he needs urgent attention. When he combines both gatheredness and separation, he is balanced and ready for other blessings. His Master empowers him, until he only sees Him. All states and their opposites become equal for him.

Know that there are three types of seekers. One type is good to creation and is weak for itself. The second type is good to itself and not to creation. The third type is good to itself and to creation and is following the proper path.

Allah has decreed that the people of humility will ultimately be mighty.

Know that the seeker has no love for the people of *Shari'a* because they are only concerned with outer knowledge.

There is nothing more beneficial to the seeker than silence, which is one of the noblest branches of serving.

It is forbidden for the seeker to speak about anything except aspects of the path, and he is only to speak a few words.

The common people avoid the wayfarers and the seekers of transformation. The common people reject *majdhubs* (ecstatics) and those who are impassioned by *Haqiqa*. Many seekers may also reject the *majdhubs*. The one who has no humility will have no might, and the one who does not give will not receive. The one who wants to receive without giving is a cheat.

Whoever finds himself in one state and does not possess its opposite, urgently needs to serve a man of Allah, and to place their affairs in his hand.

Although at the beginning the seeker may take to the path light-heartedly, he may end up with earnestness, as all things emerge from their opposites.

Give wisdom only to the seekers of wisdom, and do not conceal wisdom from them either. Yet guard your *Haqiqa* from others, lest you afflict yourself by their jealousy.

During the early stages of the seeker's learning, he tends to be concerned with the sensory world, but soon meaning follows and comes to dominate. Then the seeker prefers the company of the people of meaning and of the inner. The *himma* of the seeker will lead him to his Master, Who is the source of all meaning and of all sensory worlds.

Do not be deceived by the clothes of the wayfarer, for he may be dressed shabbily or smartly, neither of which has any relationship to his state or knowledge. He who knows may choose whatever suits him, and he who does not know must choose what is appropriate. Silence and the wearing of patched garments are attributes of service and service is the key to all openings.

The perfect seeker is like a bee, which feeds from the blossoms wherever and however it finds them.

The flowers possess the meaning and draw the seeker to their beauty. When meaning increases and is refined, it increases in honour and in value. With the sensory world, it is the opposite; when it increases in coarseness, it decreases in value.

In the seeker's early stages, his teacher is obliged to show him majesty. Beauty can bring about expansion, and that can be a fatal poison, as it is the source of all corruption. The law that governs this is mentioned in the saying, "Whoever claims to witness beauty before he has obtained *adab* by majesty is to be rejected, for he is a *dajjal* (deceiver)."

The sincere seeker has no expectation from Allah's creation and owes no debt to it. He does not see himself as wrong or a wrongdoer for he only sees Allah as the Source of his actions.

The seeker who fears creation is not a real *faqir*. If he is a real *faqir*, he will not reject anything, nor will anything frighten him. The best *faqir* is the one who trains himself in humility so that his self does not reject anything. High and low become the same for him. The mature seeker is like a hunter with a lion in his hands. He fears none of Allah's creation in the jungle. If given the choice between the garden and the fire, he would not mind choosing either.

The seeker who turns to heavenly realities after being with earthly realities is on his way to *'irfan*, and he who journeys in the opposite direction is heading for destruction. Ibn 'Ata' Allah says in his *'Hikam'*, "The goal you seek by your Lord is never held back from you, and that which you seek by yourself is ever restricted."

He who occupies himself with his body does not occupy himself with his heart, and the reverse is true. This way of Allah applies whether the occupation with the body is good or evil. When you turn to the sensory world, the meaning is still, and when you turn to the meaning, the sensory world is still. Man is constantly occupied, sometimes with the sensory world and sometimes with the world of meaning, sometimes with the inner and sometimes with the outer. He is sometimes awake and sometimes asleep.

The breaking of norms can be brought about by the seeker or by Allah's direction. From the seeker's point of view, the breaking of norms may come about through contemplation.

The seeker who is dominated by no reality other than Allah, is rejected by the common people in every instance.

Realise your attributes, and He will help you with His attributes. If you intend to reach Him by obliterating your wrong actions, you will only be disappointed.

You can only reach Him when He covers your attributes with His. This brings you to Him by what is from Him, not by what is from you.

The seeker faces ruin if he desires the love of this world, appearance, leadership, and recognition. He will only succeed if he makes humility his goal, in both the outer and the inner, both openly and privately. He must avoid turning towards creation at all costs, for that is turning away from Allah. Service is the only key to the treasures of the King. Imam al-Shadhili says, "The people (of the path) have been sentenced to humility until they become mighty, and they have been sentenced to loss until they find the Real."

Whoever plants might in the outer will reap the fruit of outer abasement. How unbecoming for him who wears the patched garment and is travelling to Allah to still desire rank and leadership in this world! Allah speaks of them in the Qur'an when He says, "Those whose striving goes astray in the life of this world while they think they are doing well."

When the *faqir* cannot find that which will expel the darkness of his heart within the permitted means, he can remove it by other means. Sometimes even *haram* things are allowed to bring back life that is slipping away.

The ordinary people detest enslavement and love freedom because slavery is abasement and freedom is might. Whoever is an *'arif*, or entrusts himself to an *'arif*, finds ease only in slavery. One who is ignorant or entrusts himself to one who is ignorant finds ease only in freedom. The *'arif* finds that all of existence serves him and he does what he wants with it. The ignorant are confused when they think themselves greater than the men of Allah and reject them. Allah says, "If you love Allah then follow the Prophet (S). Allah will love you. Understand that this world of Mine will serve the one who serves Me and will give trouble to the one who serves the world." Allah addresses the world by saying: "Oh world, serve the one who serves Me and exhaust the one who serves you."

The realised or enlightened seeker is the one who is not enamoured by the people of *Shari'a*.

When existence is in full balance within a man, Allah's perfection will manifest, and existence then becomes equal to the man and the man becomes equal to all of existence.

Humility of the outer is withdrawal, silence, little need of creation, and no reliance on them.

The real seeker is in the interspace between *Shari'a* and *Haqiqa*, and constantly taking from both oceans.

The ignorant seeker is like a piece of clay, which is covered with tar. It cannot be washed and is not good for anything.

The true seeker is like water, which flows to the lowest place and does not rise to a higher place except by force.

The ignorant seekers are worse than madmen. Sitting with an ignorant seeker is like eating poison. The ignorant *faqir* is one who is pleased with himself.

When the sensory world and the world of meaning are equal in a seeker who has turned to Allah, existence comes to his hand. The balance of the sensory world and the world of meaning is the balance between might and humility, good and evil, expansion and contraction, giving and withholding, animosity and love, nearness and distance, majesty and beauty.

The seeker is like a beginner on a hunt. If he does not make errors, he will not learn how to hit the mark. Whoever is not crooked will not be made straight. Whoever is not incorrect will not be mended. Whoever is not humble will not become mighty. Allah has sentenced the people to humility until they become mighty and only the brave become mighty.

Know that the seeker of *Haqiqa* is like the seeker of a kingdom. He who is sincere and persistent in this endeavour will become a king.

One of the signs of the outer seeker is his love for the inner, and he speaks much about the unseen. The inner seeker is in love with the outer, which is the *Shari'a* and creation. He who loves something mentions it a lot. He who mentions something that he does not possess, loves something other than it.

The Courtesies (*Adab*)

Being in service is the opposite to being one of the elite. Yet whoever seeks to be in service will find himself one of the elite. Our Prophet (S) asked to be the servant of Allah, thus the true servant of Allah's creation becomes its master.

Imitate and copy the behaviour of the great people of Allah, those who are great in their *din*, in their words and in their deeds.

When negligence occurs on the part of a Master, phenomenal afflictions come from every side to tempt and harm him because all phenomenal beings desire him. When one enters the Divine presence, a veil of light separates one from phenomenal beings and they cannot reach one. Allah says, "You will have no power over my servant."

The worst thing that can afflict the seeker is a lack of courtesy towards his parents, himself, his Shaykh and his Lord.

The level where you sit—high or low—is a reality, which influences the sensory world and the world of meaning. He (the seeker) who is sitting on the ground will have his reality higher than he who is sitting on a chair.

Sitting will bring increase in the sensory world and in the world of meaning and relates to gatheredness more than separation. The *sunna* (customary practice) of the Prophet (S) was to sit on the floor.

Whoever claims that he has drunk the drink of the wayfarers or understood their meaning and is not a *zahid* (the one who does without) in this world, has lied. As the Garden is forbidden to the one who has not died and risen, so the garden of gnosis

61

is forbidden to one whose self has not died to this world, its management and choice, its will and appetites. It is said, "Die by will, you will then be brought to life."

The source of all good things is in returning to Allah in movement and in stillness. All that appears to you of reality and fineness is by returning to Allah.

lbn 'Ata' Allah said in the *'Hikam'*, "The sign of success in the end is returning to Allah in the beginnings." He also said, "The goal which you seek by your Lord does not stop. And the goal which you seek by yourself is not easy."

lbn 'Ashir, may Allah have mercy on him, said, "Love of the life of this world is the head of every error." Another said, "The source of afflictions is love of the life of this world." The cure is only in constraint and in abstention from attachments.

Whenever your stomach is hungry, your limbs are full. Whenever your stomach is full, your limbs are hungry. The Messenger of Allah, may Allah bless him and grant him peace, related that the stomach kills intelligence. The intelligence of he who has deadened his stomach, is brought to life. Hunger is illumination for the heart and health for the body because hunger has a legacy of wisdom, and satiety has a legacy of indigestion.

Know that whenever you give goods to other than their true owners, the goods are diminished and debased because you presented them to one who did not know their value. Know that when the people of *adab* have goods and do not find one who will inspect them or who needs them, they do not demean them and offer them to one who does not recognise their value. They seal them up and keep them in their storehouses until someone who needs them comes and offers a price that pleases them.

Wilaya

The *wilaya* (the station of gnosis) is not complete for the *murid* until he reconciles two teachings: that of the elite and that of ordinary people. The latter is obtained by being with the ordinary people and seeking information.

Distinction is a result of the appropriate grooming of the *murid* and will only appear in him through knowledge, action and affirmation, not by his asking for it.

Distinction may be attained in three ways; it may be acquired, given, or inherited.

The state of distinction relates to knowledge and action, which are inseparable. Action through knowledge leads to more knowledge and greater action.

There are two types of distinction, the distinction of separation from Allah's creation and the distinction of gatheredness with *Haqiqa* and the Real.

Separation needs people, and gatheredness is needed by people. The person of separation is poor by Allah and the person of gatheredness is rich by Allah.

Know that Allah's creation is entirely founded on humility and awareness of dependency.

The gateway to awakening comes by transformation. It has two doors: *dhikr* and reflection.

Wisdom and certainty are only obtained by keeping the company of the friends of Allah. Know that whatever your *himma* connects to, will only be reached by the company of its people. It is essential on this path to recognise the people of sincerity receive confirmation from those to whom the

Beloved appears in *tajalli* (divine manifestation witnessed by the inner eye of the seeker). The friends of Allah are those who drink from the pleasure of His intimacy and He is pleased with them. They have perfected the discipline of the self and they enjoy the songs of ecstasy. They cast the eye of discrimination and reflection upon this world. The love of the Mighty Compeller overwhelms them. Goodness is obtained by whoever meets them. He said, may He be exalted! "They are few."

He said, may Allah bless him and grant him peace, "A man is on the religion (path) of his best friend." Whoever has true friendship for you, his attributes will clothe you.

Generosity with One's Self and One's Wealth

Know that money is connected to the self as the self is connected to money. Disposing of the self is like disposing of one's money. He who can spend his money liberally is not the same as he who is enslaved by it. Similarly, the one who can give of himself is not the same as the one who is obsessed with himself. What a difference between the one who controls himself and the one whose whims (and desires) control him.

Allah takes the generous one by his hand whenever he is generous. Generosity has two facets, the first relates to the self and the second relates to wealth. Generosity with the self brings mastery of inner existence, and generosity with wealth brings mastery of external existence.

When Allah wants to manifest divine generosity, Allah covers the miserliness of the servant with divine generosity and ascribes Allah's actions to the servant. Such is Allah's generosity.

The Blessing of *Dhikr*

Know that *dhikr* leads to awareness and awareness leads to knowledge and knowledge takes the seeker to the realm of withdrawal from what is other than Allah. This is the doorway to *'irfan* of Allah.

All creation is in *dhikr*. The *dhikr* of the ordinary people is separation and they are in two groups: the people of *dhikr* by the tongue, and the people of *dhikr* by the heart. The *dhikr* of the elite is gatheredness and their *dhikr* is by contemplation. The *dhikr* of the common people relates to information, whereas the *dhikr* of the elite relates to witnessing.

Dhikr is like alchemy. If you add a small amount of it to other metals, all become gold by the contact. When the false mixes with the true, all become true, and when that which is imperfect exposes itself to what is perfect it will also become perfect. When the poor connect with the rich, the poor become rich. When the powerless connects to the powerful, they also become empowered.

Allah says, "We hurl truth against falsehood and it prevails over it, and falsehood vanishes. When truth comes, falsehood departs." All of this is because Allah is most jealous. Allah does not enter into a place in which there is falsehood, unless it has been conquered and overwhelmed.

Allah says, "Call on Allah humbly and sincerely." *Dhikr* is the greatest *'ibada*. For he who is aware of what is in the hearts, the Most Generous gives divine rewards without measure.

Mankind

Spirit, Self and Body

There is no greater enemy to a man than himself. The *nafs* (the lower self) is never overcome until it knows its Master and prostrates to Him, out of fear, force, need, or love. The path is to teach the self, to groom it and to overcome its (incessant) demands.

There is no swifter way to overcome the self than by humbling it to companions. The most effective humility occurs when the self is exposed to other humble seekers.

Whoever wishes to possess creation must give generously of himself and his wealth. Know that the *ruh* comes from the world of stillness and the body from the world of toil. Allah joined them by wisdom and power. When the *ruh* dominates the body, the person is free from cares, and the reverse is true. Thus, a man always experiences two worlds: the world of rest and ease, and that of toil and difficulty.

A man in this world desires to know what lies ahead in the next world. In the next world, he desires to know what he has missed in this world. The next world is the *ruh* of this world, as this world will become the *ruh* of the next world. The *ruh* in this world hides in the body and in the next world the body will be hidden in the *ruh*. In this world, physicality dominates meaning and in the next world, meaning will dominate physicality.

Since life hides in death, death has power over life and consequently man has no rest. The opposite is also true. In the next world, when this form or body is hidden, the *ruh* is evident. In the next world, power belongs to life over death. All of this relates to Allah's perfection in making two opposites of everything, in every moment. One of two has power over the other: the next moment, the ruled becomes the ruler. This is the nature of existence.

The *arwah* (pl. of *ruh*) are one *ruh*, that is, they are all of one pattern. All essences in truth are one essence, both in separation and in gatheredness. If you look at separation, you will find separation without gatheredness, and if you look at gatheredness, you will find gatheredness without separation. When you have reflected enough however, you will find that gatheredness is nothing more than separation, and the reverse is true. When your reflection becomes perfect and established, your gatheredness will not veil you from your separation and your separation will not veil you from your gatheredness. This is the aim of contemplation.

Allah has placed the power of the body over the *ruh* in this world, as Allah has placed *Shari'a* over *Haqiqa*. The blessed Prophet (S) said, "Man will die on what he has lived and will be raised on that which he has died." Whoever is a servant of something in this world will be its servant in the next world.

He whose heart is with Allah in this world, his *ruh* will rule over his body, and his *Haqiqa* will prevail over his *Shari'a*. Such people function in this world among Allah's creation by their bodies while their hearts are totally with Allah. A great Shaykh has said, "Their bodies are in the tavern and their hearts are in the *malakut* (realm of the spiritual)."

Know that all doors between you and Allah remain locked except the door to yourself. That is why they say that he who knows himself knows his Lord. Opposing the (lower) self will enable you to win over creation, for it will then turn to you. The more you turn away from existence, the more existence will turn towards you.

Know that there is nothing worse than being obsessed with the self. Know that the root of every misfortune, negligence, and transgression is contentment with the self, whereas the root of every act of obedience and virtue relates to discontentment with the self.

Whoever wants to own existence must be generous with himself to his Lord. The generosity of Allah is such that Allah gave part of existence monetary wealth, but Allah gave all of existence the wealth that is the self.

The *ruh* is the (root of the) self, although it may vary in different states. It is as one who is called an infant or child when young and in due course becomes an old man. Similarly, the self, as long as it remains veiled in the prison of its darkness, is only the self. When it becomes free from veils and attains light and witnessing, it is the *ruh*.

Know that your essence gathers you and your attributes separate you. When separated by your essence, you are gathered by your attributes. The people of the outer love union and people of the inner are unity itself.

You will not have any peace from yourself until you withdraw into gatheredness.

The *Wali* — Man of Knowledge

The *wali* acts upon things and things do not act upon him.

The perfect *wali* is in balance between separation and gatheredness so that they are equal for him in their presence and absence.

Perfection is beyond outer separation and inner gatheredness.

When the *wali* is silent, he is the master of the world. When he speaks, existence responds to his speech. The same goes for his gatheredness, his separation, his nearness and his distance.

He possesses existence in all its attributes of expansion and contraction, good and evil, stillness and action, high and low.

The perfect *wali* is he who behaves like the weak among the strong and lowers himself from the highest stage to the lowest for the benefit of his companions. He helps the strong in their highest stages and helps the weak in their lowest stages. The Prophet (S) said, "Talk to the people according to what they understand."

The *'arif* is not an *'arif* until the suns of *'irfan* direct him to where separation and gatheredness are, and they become the same for him.

Whatever the *khalifa* wants in existence is already in existence, and whatever he does not want is not in existence, because existence is in conformity with the will of he whose will is that of Allah. He only desires what Allah desires and this fulfils him.

The station of *baqa'* (going on in Allah) is the station of the elite of the elite. It is the station of ongoingness, contentment and gain after misery and loss. Allah made the world a servant to His *khalifa*, for that is the purpose of creation to the human being. The essence of all existence emerges according to man's essence, and the attributes of all existence emerge as man's attributes. All acts of existence also emerge as man's actions. All high and low things, might, abasement, majesty, beauty and all other attributes emerge according to man's words.

All existence is in the position of *khayal* (faculty of imagination by which we render shape, form and solidity into imaginal phenomena) with man; it stands when man stands, sits when man sits and moves when he moves.

The *wali* is like the field, which remains the same whether it is winter or summer. The state of winter is that of the outer, and the state of summer is that of the inner. When the perfect balance is obtained, everything in the universe is balanced. That is Divine presence.

The *'arif* is he whose majesty is pleasing to his beauty, and whose beauty is pleasing to his majesty. He only consumes the present and this can only be when he fully owns himself.

The *wali* of the age is he whose luminosity overcomes the leaders of his time. When people of leadership surrender to him, all others surrender to him.

Meaning illumines the heart of the perfect *'arif*.

The *wali* is like cumin. He is not fragrant until crushed, either by opponents who censure him or by *waridat* (inspirations).

The action of the *'arif* shows his outer, and his word shows his inner. Neither the common people nor the elite reject his states.

The *'arif* is one who owns himself in existence and who owns existence by himself. If he wishes, he binds himself to existence, but he can also loosen this bond. The ignorant one owns himself by existence and it binds him as it wishes. The *'arif* is a master acting in his kingdom as he likes, and the ignorant one is enslaved and has no choice.

The first death of the *wali* is outer transformation and the life that follows is inner ongoingness. The second death is inner transformation and the life that follows is outer ongoingness. Outer transformation is because of inner transformation, and inner ongoingness is because of outer ongoingness. The first outer transformation is turning away from creation to Allah, followed by inner ongoingness in reaching Allah and turning back to creation. Inner transformation is joining the presence of Allah and the presence of creation. Outer ongoingness is the joining by Allah, for Allah, in Allah.

He who is by Allah acts on things and things do not act upon him.

He who does not have his *wilaya* confirmed by the common people is not a *wali*.

The Shaykh says the *wali* is like a well: those who are near it benefit, yet those who are distant benefit even more than those who are close by.

The *wali* is not perfect until he is taught three times. The first is the teaching of the parents, the second is the teaching of the shaykh and of the elite, and the third is the teaching of the common people. The teaching of the parents relates to the body, the teaching of the shaykh and the elite relates to meanings, and the teaching of the common people relates to the sensory world.

Creation either benefits you or harms you. For the *'arifs* there is only good, from evil as well as goodness. They increase by evil as they increase by good.

Part of what our Master gave me by His favour, generosity and *ihsan* (performance of good deeds, excellence, beneficence) is such that I do not remember the Prophet (S), but I find him with me (and converse with him) in the sensory world, not in the world of meaning.

Your benefit from a *wali* is according to your good opinion of him, and your loss is according to your bad opinion of him. Allah says, "I am in My servant's good opinion of Me."

When the *'arif* experiences wisdom, its opposite appears to him. He recognises the wisdom of finding and of losing, of constriction and of expansion, of love and of animosity, of the seen and the unseen, of manifestation and of concealment, of hunger and of fullness, of poverty and of wealth. The same is true for all opposites. Man's existence bases itself on this wisdom.

Know that the perfect *wali* of Allah is present in every presence.

Knowledge is gnosis of the art and it is not the art. Action is the art itself. *Himma* is the root of action and its branches.

The perfect *'arif* uses existence in all its states. When he is in a state of gatheredness, he uses the power of gatheredness. When he is in a state of separation, he uses separation as wisdom. If he does not use it by wisdom, he uses it by power.

Creation does not veil him from Allah's presence, and Allah's presence does not veil him from creation, for he sees the Master in every state.

Praise and censure are equal to the *wali*, as is giving and withholding or the presence of an enemy or a lover.

The corruption of the heart is due to perceiving other than Him. The corruption of the body is due to adding food to food. The *murid* seeks to live, being pleased with himself. The perfect *wali* has finished discounting himself and is present with his Master in all states. He is absent, present, travelling, resident. His separation does not veil him from his gatheredness and his gatheredness does not veil him from his separation. All opposites are equal to him. He is the true servant and therefore he is a true master.

Man's Position in Creation

Man is a copy of existence and existence is a copy of man. All opposites meet in the human being.

Man is always interacting, always residing with the inner and the outer. Either gathered or separated, he is near or far, small or great, high or low, and he relates to the sensory world, or to the world of meaning, majesty or beauty, life or death, movement or stillness.

All phenomenal beings in existence are in love with man and seek him out for his evolved consciousness.

Whoever owns his self owns all existence, and whoever is owned by his self is owned by existence.

Man has no greater enemy than the self. If he overcomes the self, he is the master, and if he does not, he is owned by everything.

Prostate yourself to the One Master with fear or force or longing or love! You can never be content or pleased as long as you do not witness your Master.

Know that, in truth, all of existence is from you and you are from it. According to the degree of sincerity in your service to Allah, Allah's creation will serve you and will reward you according to the extent that you are its master.

Commensurate with your gratitude in thanking creation, creation will thank you. Commensurate with your despising and criticising it, it will despise and criticise you. Commensurate with how generous you are to it, it is generous to you. Commensurate with how miserly you are to it, it is miserly to you.

Allah has made the human being the master of all existence and the sultan of His Divine kingdom. Existence connects to him, is humble before him, loves him and obeys his commands and prohibitions.

Outer blessings are never complete for any man until they become inner blessings, and vice versa. Sensory blessings are never enough for any man until they become blessings of meaning and the reverse is true.

When you are just to all of existence and what it contains, it will be just to you.

He who is looking for the fruits of meaning and knowledge, is not concerned with the fruits of the sensory. Meaning overcomes some people and the sensory world overcomes others.

Allah's perfection shows in the human being, as he changes in states and attributes. He experiences good and evil, outer and inner, height and depth, the sensory world and the world of meaning. The good in these states turns him from good and joins him to evil, and the evil in these states turns him from evil towards good. The reverse is true of the opposite states. The good in them turns him from evil and joins him to good, and the evil in them turns him from good and joins him to evil.

The son of Adam is the *khalifa* of Allah on this earth. Whoever serves the *khalifa* serves Allah. "Those who pay allegiance to you are really paying allegiance to Allah, and the power of Allah is above all hand."

The ongoingness of man in this existence is founded on variety and differences. He who stays in one state longer than another will only be corrupted and destroyed.

Everything in creation is at the very limit of wonder and beauty. All that is in existence is within you. Existence will continue due to differentiation and the action of opposites. Existence will decrease with lack of variation and differentiation.

Man is always changing and residing with the inner or the outer. He is either gathered or separated. He is near or far, small or great, high or low, relating to the sensory world or to the world of meaning, to majesty or beauty, is alive or dead, and experiences movement or stillness.

The blessed Prophet (S) said, "Allah has created Adam in His likeness." Allah created man with his inner gatheredness and outer separation, the same as this existence. Man's separation grows from his gatheredness, and the reverse is true. When man is content with his heart, he reaches the conclusion of Ibn Mashish, who says, "I have washed myself of my knowledge and action, so that I own neither action nor knowledge." Thus, for the human, the path to perfection lies in the breaking of norms, and only the steadfast ones can do this by keeping the company of the elite.

The habit of the self is to desire anything it can obtain. When the self is prevented from obtaining something, yearning and passion increase.

Allah has made the human being a copy of existence and existence a copy of Himself. He placed darkness and light in existence and in man. When darkness appears, light is hidden, and the reverse is true, both in existence and in man. Whenever the outer is illumined, the inner is dark, and whenever the inner is illumined, the outer is dark. Whoever thinks that the luminosity of the outer demands the luminosity of the inner is ignorant. Man has two worlds, outer and inner, and the outer world is the opposite of the inner.

Know that the heart of a man is like a king's village. No village can have two rulers in it, and either the inner or the outer rules the heart. These two opposites never rule together in the heart at one time. Whenever they meet, the one drives the other out. The heart is never free from either of these two rulers who have their own armies and emissaries.

Know that all things, good or evil, yearn for man and wish to belong to him, and they do not depart until he takes from them what pleases him. As long as man is in this world, everything good and evil yearns for him and craves for him.

There are two types of knowledge: outer knowledge, which is by repetition, and inner knowledge, which is divine and reflects the Prophetic revelations. Inner knowledge is not by imitation, but is based on the tree of *iman*, which grows in the heart. Its root and branches are in the heavens. This is the Garden of the sincere and it is Allah's Garden in this world. Whoever enters it does not yearn for the Garden of the next world.

The heart of man has only one direction. When he neglects his outer, his inner turns to him. When he neglects his inner, his outer turns to him.

The Adamic being is the groom of this kingdom and all phenomenal beings honour him, seek him, and desire him, both in the outer and in the inner. When man turns to outer things, they take him, enter his heart, and boast about him to inner things. Then the inner follows. When he neglects outer things and turns to the inner things, they besiege or seize him and boast of him to the outer things. Then the outer things follow him. All creation follows his scent.

My Master gave me two worlds, the world of the sensory, and the world of meaning. He placed them like brides, both of whom desire me. When one of them obtains me, she boasts proudly to the other, but they are both under my command. When I turn to the world of the sensory, it instantly obeys my command, without hesitation. Similarly, when I turn to the world of meaning, I am the prince and creation is my servant, and that is from Allah's bounty.

Types of People

Generally, there are three types of people: the common people. who are the ones who love *Shari'a*, the elite who are in *Shari'a* but love *Haqiqa*, and the elite of the elite who are in *Haqiqa* but love *Shari'a*. These three types are easily differentiated by their actions. The common people act by imitation, the distinguished ones act by love and evidence, and the elite of the elite act by contemplation and witnessing.

The people of this world, whose sensory world dominates the world of meaning, have darkness dominating their luminosity. As for those of the other world, the world of meaning dominates the sensory world and their luminosity dominates their darkness.

Kingdoms are of three types. The first is the kingdom of the people of this world who are the people of fear and hope. The second kingdom is of the people of the next world, who are the people of yearning and love. The third kingdom is of the people of Allah and they are between the *'kaf'* and the *'nun'* (*'kun'* is the command 'to be'). The kingdom of the people of this world is Allah's creation for creation, and with creation. The kingdom of the people of the next world is Allah's creation for Allah. The kingdom of the people of Allah is by Allah, for Allah, and in Allah.

The common people are those whom gatheredness separates. The elite are those who gather after separation and the elite of the elite are those who separate after being gathered.

The common people say that they are the people of the outer and there is no God but Him. The elite say that they have no strength and no power except from Him. The elite of the elite say there is no blessing except from Him and nothing exists except Him. Allah was and there was nothing with Him, and He is now as He was before.

Those that turn to Allah are in two groups: the people of means and the people of divestment. The first group are the people of *Shari'a*, and the second group are the people of *Haqiqa*. In the first group, *Shari'a* dominates, and in the second group, *Haqiqa* dominates.

The ascetic people of divestment are concerned with contemplating Allah's attributes and essence.

For the people of Allah, all things and their opposites are equal: sweetness and bitterness, good and evil, giving and keeping, life and death. They obtain the benefit of evil as they obtain the benefit of good. They withdraw from everything and are present in everything. Allah says of them in a *hadith qudsi*, (tradition or report in which Allah speaks in the first person through the tongue of the Prophet Muhammed) "I become the hearing by which he hears and the sight by which he sees."

The people who use the self are in two groups. Those of the first group have luminosity of the self, and they are looking for the outer. Those of the second group are dark and are connected to the outer. The people of light are with light and the people of darkness are in darkness. All is from Him, by Him, unto Him.

There are only four groups of people. Two relate to outer knowledge and the other two to inner knowledge. They are the people of the outer sensory world and the world of outer meaning and the inner sensory world and the world of inner meaning.

"Allah has bought from the *mu'mins* their selves and for this, they have the Garden." The people of the outer understand this to be the Garden of the next world, whereas the people of the inner understand this to be the garden of witnessing in this world and the next. Ibn 'Ata' Allah says, "Allah has a Garden in this world. Whoever enters it does not yearn for any aspect of the next world. What a difference between the seekers of gardens and he who seeks the Creator of this world and the next!"

The fruits of the trees of the outer are the inner and vice versa. The fruits increase until they are developed and completed. The results of the outer are the inner, and the results of the inner are the outer. The trees become fruit and the fruits become trees.

The outer of the people of the outer is their inner and the inner of the people of the inner is their outer. The custom of Allah is that things hide in their opposites.

The outer is the source of the inner, and the inner is the source of the outer. Separation is the source of gatheredness and gatheredness is the source of separation.

The man of the outer plants gatheredness and separation grows for him. The man of the inner plants separation and gatheredness grows for him.

Allah brings forth the living from the dead and the dead from the living.

The people of the outer broadcast their words with good intentions, while the people of the inner conceal their words, but their actions show their good intentions.

The *Shari'a* of the people of the outer is words, but their reality is their actions. The people of the inner have ninety-nine divisions of action and one of words, and the people of the

82

outer are the reverse. Action relates to doing and words relate to knowledge.

The people of witnessing are in three groups. The first group sees action emanating from this world. The second group see that action belongs to power. The third group sees action belonging to the All-Powerful, from Him unto Him. In the first group are the common people, veiled from themselves by creation. In the second group are people of *Iman*, veiled by power from the All-Powerful, and in the third group are the people of Allah, annihilated from other-than-Him. They only see the One, for there is none other-than-Him.

For the common people, all that is beautiful is acceptable and all that is ugly is objectionable. With the elite, whatever brings them to Allah is acceptable and whatever distracts them from Allah is objectionable, even though it may appear acceptable to the common people. As for the elite of the elite, all that exists is acceptable for they recognise Allah in every state and do not reject Him.

When you do well by the common people, they repay you with evil, and when you do evil, they repay you with evil, because the outer dominates them. When the wayfarer does good to the elite of the elite, they do good to him, and when he does evil, they do good to him, because they have withdrawn to Allah, and whatever comes to them they consider as good coming from Him.

The common people are in the prison of norms, bound and fettered. The breaking of norms has four aspects. It is by heartfelt yearning, by great fear, by force, or by norms that are broken for them without their ever knowing.

Whoever has norms broken for him, and recognises how they are broken, he is the *'arif* of Allah.

Creation divides into two groups, people who own wealth and people who own themselves.

The common people are content with themselves. One says to the other, "I am better than you," and that is because the (lower) self is alive. The elite see the others as better than they are because their selves are dead.

The nearness of the ordinary people to Allah is with respect to their actions and their distance is with respect to their *himma*. The distance of the elite of the elite is in their nearness and the reverse is true. Their gatheredness is in their separation and the reverse is true. Their transformation is in their going-on and the reverse is true.

For the people of the outer, a community enriches a man, though one man does not enrich a community. As for the people of the inner, one man enriches a community and the community does not enrich a man.

Those that relate to Allah are of two groups: those who are poor in Allah and those who are rich in Allah. That which is appropriate for the poor is not appropriate for the rich, and vice versa. Nothing harms those who are poor in Allah more than management and choice, and nothing benefits them more than lack of management and choice. For those who are rich in Allah the reverse is true. Nothing harms the poor in Allah like expansion, and nothing benefits them like constriction. For those who are rich in Allah the reverse is true. Nothing harms the poor as much as occupation with creation and nothing benefits them more than occupation with their selves. As for the rich in Allah, nothing harms them more than occupation with their selves, and nothing benefits them as much as occupation with creation. Glory be to the One Who created all in its opposites! Blessings for some are afflictions for others.

Know that the people of servitude divide into two groups. One group serves Allah in fear and awe, and another group serves Him in yearning, passion, and love. As for the people of fear and awe, their way is, "He knows so He exists" and the way of the people of yearning and love is, "He exists so He knows."

There is no vanity in the one who wears the patched robe and fasts the day and rises in the night and keeps the company of those in this state. Vanity is from the one who wears fine clothes, does not fast in the day, sleeps the night, and keeps the company of those in this state. The one who leaves this world is not *zahid* in it. The one who is *zahid* in this world is the one who keeps its company. The one who finds this world and then abandons it is not *zahid* in it. The one who is *zahid* in this world is the one for whom its existence and absence are the same. The one who leaves this world and leaves its people is not *zahid* in it. The one who is *zahid* in this world is the one who recognises Allah in its retreat and advance.

The people of meaning travel by attributes, and the ascetic people of divestment travel by essence. When the humility of the people of meaning is in the meaning, their striving is in the essence. When the humility of the ascetic people of divestment is in the sensory world, their striving is in the meaning.

Sensory striving always brings constriction, whereas striving in meaning always brings expansion. Striving in meaning is gatheredness and the joy of expansion in it continues. He who strives at the sensory level is continually in constriction.

The seeker on the path of asceticism is always in retreat, prayer, fasting, abasement, recitation of the Qur'an during the day, silence, lowering his gaze, sitting with the man of Allah and fearfully desiring the knowledge of Allah.

To serve is majesty, and it is the door to beauty.

Retreat, which is *i'tikaf* (temporary retreat), is a tree, and all the attributes of serving are its branches.

The Heart

Allah has given the human being two types of *himma*: one is in the heart, and the other in the body. The *himma* of the heart is above that of the body. The Prophet (S) said, "There is a lump within the body of the son of Adam. When it is sound, the entire body is sound, when it is sick, the entire body is sick. It is the heart." Allah says in a *hadith qudsi*, "Neither My heavens nor My earth contain Me, but the heart of the *mu'min* contains Me." The Prophet (S) said, "Allah provides for His servant according to his *himma*."

The heart is the house of Allah. From it come the actions of the world, whether good or evil. If beauty appears in your heart in the outer, existence will confront you with beauty.

The scope of all of existence is in the heart of the son of Adam because his noble heart contains the lights of *Haqiqa* and its secrets.

Reading books does not cure hearts. Their medicine lies in the company of the masters of hearts (the gnostics). Books are only the residue from the knowledge of hearts; they are merely an indication. Books help man when he does not see the Beloved. When he sees Him, he writes books.

Nothing holds you away from Allah except your pre-occupations, which distract you from Him. Nothing distracts you from the house of the Beloved other than pre-occupation with love itself, rather than with the Beloved. The people of the outer are only free in the outer, but the people of the inner are free in the worlds of both the inner and the outer.

I asked the Shaykh one day about the hardness of my heart, the cause of which I did not know. The Shaykh answered, "It is because you have been mixing with the dead." I asked him,

"Who are the dead?" He said, "They are the worldly people. I did not mean that you aimed for them, but simply by being with them, by joining with them, harm comes to you because of their nature. If you want the cure, you must keep the company of the people of Allah, of whom worldly people are suspicious. Keep their company and you will be cured."

Someone said to his teacher, "I love you." The teacher said, "What have you done for me with your love, because love without sacrifice is hypocrisy." My Shaykh said, advising me, "My son, if you want to reach the Master, be the servant of His servant and do not desire to be His servant directly." The blessed Prophet (S) said, "Know that the human being is like a chameleon, he never alights on anything but that he takes its colour."

States and Stations

Abasement, Humility, and Might

Outer might can only emerge from inner humility, and inner might emerges from outer humility.

Bistami said that Allah revealed to him that, "if you want Us, you must have humility." Abbas Mursi said, "This path of ours can only be travelled by people who will sweep the dung from the roads with their souls. The song says, "Humble yourself before the One you love, for passion is not easy. If the Beloved is pleased, then arrival is assured. Humble yourself to Him and you will come to see His beauty."

There is a big difference between acquired humility and compulsory humility. Whoever comes to humility by choice, might will come to him by force, and vice versa.

If you plant humility in service, you will find yourself a free king, and if you plant freedom and might, you will find yourself an old servant. What you plant is what you yourself harvest. Knowledge is the reason for control of everything and its key is to sit with the *'arifs* of Allah. The same is true regarding the key of ignorance. It is acquired by sitting with the ignorant.

There is no act of disobedience that returns you to humility and repentance before your Master but that it is better than an act of obedience by which the self exalts itself. This is because when you are the slave of obedience, you are the slave of obedience. When you are the slave of disobedience, you are the slave of disobedience. When you are the slave of Allah, loyal to Him, be His slave in every situation in which He places you. You are part of His domain. He does what He wants in His domain. He is the just Judge

Who commands and cannot be commanded. He manages time and space. He is the Creator of everything in existence. He knows what is best for His creation and what misleads them. All that emanates from Allah is perfect and complete.

Freedom and Enslavement

Whoever comes to service by choice, freedom will come to him by necessity, and vice versa.

Servitude is essential for the beginner and is demanded from him until his end, which is his transformation. The wisdom of this is that the end is the manifestation of the beginning.

Men's honour is in serving, and it involves two aspects: enslavement of the sensory world and enslavement of the world of meaning. When he comes to the end of the world of meaning, he is lost in the sensory world. They alternate like winter and summer.

There are two conditions for freedom. The first is humility of the self and the weakening of it, and the second is constant *dhikr* of Allah.

True humility is to the Master and Lord of all creation, who will free the seeker from enslavement to himself? Bad courtesy to the real people of Allah may appear as freedom and may bring about might, but it will surely not lead to humility.

Service is of four types. One may be a servant of oneself, a servant of wealth, a servant of the people and this world, or a servant of Allah.

Whatever you seek, you become its servant. If you are the servant of Allah, you will only seek those who will join you with your Master.

He who flows with the changes that come upon him is free, whereas he who is reliant on things is their servant and existence owns him.

When the servant is empowered by the Master people despise and belittle him and when they are under his power they exalt and respect him.

There are two wines: the wine of humility, which is majesty, and the wine of freedom, which is beauty.

Whoever is described by the attributes of humility serves his Master at every stage, thus everything serves him. As for the one who is described by the attributes of the Master, he serves himself, thus everything flees from him. These are the people of the veil. People of the veil are with their own will, and the people of witnessing are with the will of their Lord.

Whenever you desire anyone other than your Master, you are his or her servant. Whenever you see the benefit or harm in anyone other than your Master, you are his servant. Whenever you are humble to anyone other than your Master, you are his servant. Whenever you rely on anyone other than your Master, you are his servant. Whenever you are terrified of anyone other than your Master, you are his servant. Whenever you ask for help of anyone other than your Master, you are his servant.

Know that it is impossible to separate enslavement from freedom. In this regard, there are three sorts of people. The first group of people are of the station of annihilation in Allah. Their freedom is in their inner and their enslavement is in their outer. They are the people of the inner of the *din*. The second group of people are of the station of the beginning. They are the reverse of the first group and they are the people of the outer of this world. Their enslavement is in their inner and their (apparent) freedom is in their outer. The third group are the leaders of the common people. Their enslavement is in the inner and their (apparent) freedom is in the outer.

Part of the custom of Allah in existence is that existence confronts man with whatever is in his heart. He said, may He be exalted! "If He knows that there is goodness in your heart, He will give you better than that which you love." The first group, the people of annihilation, confront existence with their hearts filled with freedom, so existence confronts them with freedom. They find the people of heaven and earth free. For that reason, you find them rejected by all creation.

The people of the second group, the beginners on the path of poverty, confront existence with their hearts filled with enslavement to Allah, so existence confronts them with enslavement. Therefore, they find all the people of the earth to be their slaves. It is related in a *hadith* (tradition or report narrating the deeds or utterances of the Prophet Muhammad and his companions), "O world! Serve whoever serves Me, and exhaust whoever serves you!" For that reason, you find this group accepted by all creation.

Expansion and Constriction

The greatest misfortune of the outer is expansion, and the greatest misfortune of the inner is constriction.

When people of the inner experience outer constriction, they increase in inner expansion. When people of the outer, increase in the outer expansion, they increase in inner constriction.

My Shaykh advised me and said, "My son, do not choose one state over another. Be with that in which Allah establishes you. If you have any choice then choose constriction over expansion, for the source of inner expansion is outer constriction. Read what Allah says: 'We sent it (outer constriction) down on the Night of Power and what do you know about the Night of Power?'"[8]

---

8   One of the odd nights in the last ten days of Ramadan, the Night of Power or Determination signifies the occasion of the revelation of the whole Qur'an to the Prophet Muhammad (S) as well as a time when the affairs of the next year are determined for the believer.

Stations

The Shaykh said, "My Master gave me the ability to pardon myself and pardon whoever pardons me, and whoever does not pardon me. He made me sometimes free and sometimes a servant, sometimes man and sometimes woman, and made me change in all conditions to obtain all desires. Sometimes I am old, sometimes a child, and sometimes obedient, sometimes rebellious. I am in the highest high and the lowest low, I am born rich and poor, certain and weak, destitute in the house, lower than the seventh earth. The cosmos is in my hand and I am driven away in my humility. I am a madman among the people of the earth. I am a star and nothing among the people of *'irfan*. I am drowned in darkness by others. These are but some of my attributes and states."

Whoever is not in increase must be in decrease, except for the one who has sincerely turned to Allah. For him increase is increase, and decrease is increase. However, for he who turns to other than Allah, his increase is decrease and his decrease is also decrease.

Conduct

Allah provides for His servant according to his *himma* (resolute yearning). Allah helps His creation by what they seek. He helps those who seek the Name with the Name, He helps those who seek His attributes with attributes and He helps those who seek His essence with essence. The extent of each is according to the *himma* of the individual.

Openings occur according to the *himma* of the being and the rewards are according to that being's strength. As the self has come from the Real, if its direction is sound, its *'irfan* is sound. Once that knowledge is established, suspension of that knowledge is forbidden for people of the path. Whoever you abase yourself to, be he a king or a servant, he will be abased to you.

There are two *himmas*: The first relates to the outer and the second to the inner. The *himma* of the outer is action based on what you know, and the *himma* of the inner is your steadfast knowledge of certainty. When your two *himmas* combine, be sure that the thing you are pursuing will occur.

Whoever confirms the norms will find the norms, and whoever rejects norms, norms will reject him. Whoever confirms breaking of norms will find breaking of norms. You do not turn to a thing, but Allah helps you in it and for it. Help is not withheld by your Master until your *himma* ends.

Good opinion ennobles he who holds it. Allah says, "I am with My servant's good opinion of me." He who thinks of beauty will find beauty. The good opinion of Allah and good opinion of the servants of Allah are the two greatest qualities. Whoever thinks good thoughts and speaks good words or carries out good action will find good, and vice versa.

Embellishments

Encounters and Stories

Imam al-Shafi'i asked his teacher, Imam Malik, "Do I stop at what I've taken from you and restrict myself to it, or do I do *ijtihad* (an exercise of reason to establish the ruling of *Shari'a* on a given point)?" Imam Malik's answer was, "My son, make *ijtihad*."

The Shaykh asked his *murid*, "Why don't you make a sound or announce yourself before you come in?" The *murid* replied that he was shy. The Shaykh explained that he (the Shaykh) is like a mother to her baby. When the baby begins to cry milk starts to build up in the mother's breast. "In the same way when I hear your voice, I am ready to give you nourishment."

Someone asked Imam 'Ali, "O Master, did you come to know Allah by Muhammad or did you come to know Muhammad by Allah?" Imam Ali replied, "Had I known Allah by Muhammad, I would not have been able to cross over to Him. Allah has enabled me to know Allah by Allah's self. Allah will not be known by man. It is man who will be known by Allah."

I told my Shaykh that I am weak when it comes to words, but strong in action. My Shaykh said, "Praise be to Allah that you recognise His favours to you, for had He placed the power which He placed in your action in your words, the ordinary people would have destroyed you. You can be safe, but not from the *ulama* (people of outer knowledge)."

The Shaykh used to treat most illnesses of the outer with oils and most illnesses of the body with milk. He used to pray holding the remedy, asking Allah to put *baraka* (blessing, grace) and healing in it.

There was a woman washing her clothes on a riverbank. Her small child suddenly fell in the water and vanished from her sight. She fled to the Shaykh, striking her head and increasing her screaming when the Shaykh's companions informed her they could not swim. The Shaykh told her that if she was truthful about her desperation, she should go back to the riverbank and she would find her child safe. She returned and saw the child safe on the other side. The woman was sincere in the eye of the Shaykh, and Allah confirmed that it is Allah Who rescues the desperate when Allah is truly called upon.

Abul-Hassan al-Shadhili went to a king of this world in order to make a request in answer to the needs of certain people but his request was not granted. He went back and forth eighteen times and finally his request was granted. This is an example of persistence and certainty when facing Allah's test.

A man came to Imam al-Junayd and said, "Praise be to Allah" and Imam al-Junayd reminded him to finish it with the "Lord of the worlds." The man answered, "What value is there that the worlds have to be connected with Him?" Imam al-Junayd said to him, "When that which is in time is connected to that which is out of time, that which is of time vanishes and that which is out of time goes on."

Know that Allah has created existence for His perfect lovers. They are the ones who are not distracted from their Beloved in this world or the next. Allah has created the earth for His lovers' sake. Had it not been for them, He would not have created existence. Allah has created the *jinn* (creatures made of fire) and the angels for their sake. Allah has created the sun, moon and stars for their sake. Allah has created the seas, rivers, fish and beasts for their sake. Allah has created hundreds of mercies for their sake. They are the lovers of Allah. They are His pure servants. They are the people of Allah and His party. They are the *awliya'* and they are the people of His Presence. All of these people also cling to the Messenger of Allah and drink from his continuous fountain. Had it not been for the beloved Muhammad (S), this world and its people would not have existed.

Counsel

Whoever is ungrateful for his Creator's blessings risks receiving any blessings.

Do not deny the virtue of the ordinary people. Allah may open the door for you through one of them. The Shaykh relates that it was an ordinary person who took him to the door and handed him the key. This person had abandoned it because he did not know how to use the key to open the door. The Shaykh relates that he used the key and the door opened for him. That is what the Shaykh calls the door of transformation. The one who opens it cannot deny it, nor can he deny the virtue of the teacher who shows him the way to ongoingness.

Perhaps Allah will shower His mercy upon the servant who is rebellious and may punish the one who is obedient. How can a true servant ever rely on his own obedience or disobedience?

The servant is to rely on the One Who created his obedience and his rebellion.

Abdul Qadir al-Jilani says, "I came to all the doors of Allah and found crowds of people around the doors, until I reached the door of humility and poverty. This door was not crowded, so I entered. I turned back to look and found all the other doors still crowded."

Know that Allah is most jealous and does not enter the heart of he who has anything else in his heart.

Know that the blessings that come to you from a state of constriction and humility are a hundred times greater than the blessings that come to you from a high state.

Low things are the roots of all high things.

You bestow yourself on Him and He bestows all existence on you. He created you before you came into existence and He gave you the ability to have power over it.

The word of a man is like his daughter. The man only mirrors his daughter and is kind to her.

The Shaykh advised me and said, "My son, I moved freely in the land and did not find anything more profitable or swift than change. The pleasure of passion is only in change, and the goal of love is to be coloured by change."

If you have not tasted what the real people of *'irfan* have tasted, it is because you are deprived of that taste, and because of your love of this world you are veiled. This relates to when he said, "Make me live as a *miskin* (destitute or indigent person) and die as a *miskin* and gather me in the company of the *masakin* (plural of *miskin*)."

Ibn al-Farid says, "The most wondrous thing is that whenever I increase in my abasement to the people, my power among them rises."

The Shaykh says, "The one who is distracted is not one of us."

Know that there is nothing more beautiful than the assemblies of the *fuqara'* and those who are seeking the Face of Allah. Whoever considers himself independent is at a loss. Allah guides those who are guided by Him. Those who are content with themselves have no entitlement to increase. Whenever increase is absent, decrease appears.

There are four types of recommendation. The first is intense silence, the second is lowering the eyes, the third is generosity of the hand, and the fourth is sitting with the men of knowledge.

These are outer majestic realities and they are the keys to inner beauty.

An *'arif* gave advice to his companion, "O my son, be aware of the company of three types of people. The first are heedless tyrants, the second are negligent reciters (of the Qur'an), and the third are ignorant Sufis. The ignorant Sufi is uglier than the first two because the harm of the others will come to you in small doses, whereas that of the ignorant Sufi is like deadly poison—it kills immediately."

Be among the wise who act by wisdom in the state of separation and by power in the state of gatheredness.

Connect your gatheredness and sever your separation. Allah is the light and He is seen only by the one whose heart is filled with light. Whenever there is gatheredness in the heart, there is outer separation.

This world is like a corpse and its people are like the dogs who attend it. To be distinguished is to be diverted from it and elevated by *himma* from its people.

The diligent seeker is the one who keeps constant company with the people of Allah. Whoever does not sit with the men of Allah has missed the opportunity and is an outcast.

Whoever sees the world by the world, his inner eye is blind, and whoever sees the world by its Maker is indeed witnessing the truth.

The Shaykh said, "O my son, you must keep the company of great people and be near them. Be close to the leaders of the outer and the leaders of the inner. Know that our occupation is like gold, the more you rub it, the more it is enhanced.

The Shaykh said, "My son, when you desire the results of the outer, water it with the inner and it will grow. When you desire the inner, water it with the outer and it will be established. The outer can never exist without the inner, and if it does it will be imperfect, because all things are only established by their opposites."

The right way is to turn away from the ordinary people, so that you do neither good nor evil with them but are occupied with the Master of all people. By turning to creation for good or for evil you have turned away from your Master. Leave creation, including yourself, to the One Who created it. The source of rescue and success is occupation with Him. Whatever distracts you from your Master is only an idolatrous image. The worst distractions of all are anxiety about provision and fear of creation.

Allah is the Most Generous and He brought you into existence as a favour and when you return this favour, which is not yours, He will take your attributes and replace them with His.

Whenever you turn to your Master with might, He binds you to humility, and vice versa. Whenever you turn to the servants of Allah with humility, you see your Master in them and Allah will fulfil your needs immediately, because your turning to them by Him is your turning to Him by them.

Guard yourself, guard the rest of mankind and guard your contemplation of your Lord. Be a seeker and do not be sought. Be a lover and do not be desired.

An atom of action of the heart is better than a mountain of actions of the limbs.

Prophetic advice is that a dirham from trade is better than ten dirhams in fixed wage, because the world only increases through people of trade.

The Shaykh says, "Ration your words and your supplication will be answered."

The Shaykh's advice is that, "When you hesitate about something or need something, aim for its source or its people."

The place of man's healing is the place of his breaking, and no greater healing takes place than the breaking of the self. There is no healing for man nearer and greater than the healing of his self. The higher self is the most hostile of enemies and the most beloved of lovers.

Seek uprightness and do not seek generous gifts, because the seeker of uprightness is drawn to perfection, whereas the seeker of generous gifts is drawn to error. Seeking a portion of the generous gifts distracts you from Allah. It is bad *adab* with Him and the path is entirely *adab*. Allah says regarding the Qur'an, "Only the purified shall touch it." Ibn 'Ata' Allah says, "Your turning to creation is your turning away from Allah."

Advice from the Shaykh is that when someone comes to you seeking a need from Allah and from you, make an agreement appropriate to your understanding. Ask him for a written testimony before a witness and if you find this written testimony real, then make the agreement. Otherwise, do not. Never make an agreement with anyone unless it is in writing, and you are fully content with it, otherwise the outcome will be wrong.

If you hear something and do not understand it, do not compare it with what you have in yourself. Keep it apart until you understand it and when you need it benefits will come to you.

Know that concern about provision is the biggest thing that comes between the seeker and what he truly seeks.

Do not reject any of the states in which Allah has put you. Part of what my Shaykh has advised me is not to put myself in a position where I feel imposed upon. Our path does not bring about burdens (worldly imposition).

Know that the keys to the unseen lie with outer constriction and afflictions. Ibn 'Ata' Allah says, "Great afflictions are celebrated by those who know." Had man recognised the benefits of needs it would have sufficed for him to have reached the ultimate Truth. It is said that need is a copy of the great name of Allah.

The Shaykh told me that when your opinion of anyone is good, then your opinion of yourself is good, and vice versa. If you are generous to someone, then you are generous to yourself. If you deprive someone, then you deprive yourself. If you elevate someone, then you elevate yourself. If you are a lover of the servants of Allah, then you are a lover of yourself. The Shaykh told me not to look at any creation, for a glance at creation will separate you from Allah. Creation is like water in a valley. If you cross the valley and prolong looking at the water while you are crossing, your vision will be scattered. It is like that with creation. Beware of looking at it. Goodness lies in withdrawal from creation. The virtues of withdrawal, if listed, would fill what is between the heavens and the earth.

When you examine knowledge, you will find that its source is ignorance, and the reverse is true. Knowledge is a proof of essence and veils it. Ignorance is a proof of attributes and veils them.

The Shaykh says, "Wisdom comes to its owner from the presence of might."

If you want to see wonders, you should work wonders. Otherwise, you are like the one who plucks grapes from thorns.

Whoever rebels while remembering Allah is better than the one who does not rebel and does not remember Allah.

Free this world from your hands and be patient in being done with it. It will then leave your heart. When it has left your heart and is in your hand it will not harm you.

Know that occupation with the Beloved is the desire and the goal. When people are absorbed with *'ibada*, absorb yourself with the Object of *'ibada*. When people are absorbed with love, absorb yourself with the Beloved. When people are absorbed with *du'a* (supplicating Allah) absorb yourself with the One to whom *du'a* is addressed. When people are absorbed with enemies, absorb yourself with love of the Beloved.

Wisdom (*Hikma*)

The enlightened person tells his son to travel and find teachers because he has concern for him and if one has too much concern for one's pupil, the pupil will not learn. The father tells his son, "Find someone to teach you wisdom and stay with him." After some time, the son returns to his father and says, "I have learnt not to be involved with that which does not concern me." The father says, "You still have one thing to learn", and sends the son away again. The son returns after some time and says that he has not found that for which he was sent and begs his father to tell him. The father says, "Always be very close to the wise ones."

The enmity of a person who is intelligent and full of desires is sweeter and more pleasant than the friendship of an ignorant person.

You will find ultimately that you can only see by Him and from Him.

You are ever changing, and He is the same. You may know this, or you may not know it; every moment your state evolves.

The reason for a person's involvement with existence is his love for existence and its enslavement of him, whereas both are servants to Allah.

Allah has said that he who has been given wisdom has been given much good.

Your Lord's generosity is that whether you turn your *himma* to a good or to an evil thing, He helps you and supports you, and prepares you for it. Allah, glory be to Him, says, "Whoever draws near me a hand's length, I draw near him an arm's length."

Your self is only owned by you through the *'irfan* of Allah. Otherwise, when your self owns you, you are the servant of existence.

Humble yourself before the One you love, and you will reach your goal.

The light of meaning alone can soften and nourish your heart.

Man understands the answer to a question according to his sincerity.

I guarantee intimacy (closeness to Allah) for whoever drowns and does not struggle. The lack of struggle is victory over the self. Whoever does not aid the self, Allah aids him.

You only find yourself in the place where you are.

The self's habits stop it trying to find anything new, for it is usually content with what it has and wants to stay that way.

If you increase your *zuhud* in what you have, His gifts to you will grow without end, until your *himma* ceases.

When you want gatheredness, connect yourself to separation and stay there. Gatheredness will seek you, and the reverse is true.

He who has truly attained the *Haqiqa* of awareness has no need of any creature in existence, for he is a living *ruh* by his Master. He is called "Ibrahimian" because Jibril came to the Prophet Ibrahim (Pbuh) (Abraham) when a catapult set up by the idol worshippers of his city was hurling him into the fire and asked him, "Have you any needs from Allah?" and the Prophet Ibrahim replied by saying, "No, I do not need to ask Him for anything for He has full knowledge of my situation."

He who is ignorant of himself is ignorant of his Lord. Know that the place of knowledge is in the inner and the place of action is in the outer, and there is a big difference between reporting an action and taking part in it.

Speech is the juncture of the outer and the inner.

Knowledge emerges from action and action emerges from knowledge, as if knowledge hides in action and action hides in knowledge. Allah manifests Himself to people of knowledge and to people of ignorance. The *'arif* recognises Him in every instance and confirms His Oneness while the ignorant reject Him. Thus, creation will reject the ignorant and they will reject themselves. Had they been able to confirm themselves, they would have confirmed their Lord. Had they confirmed their Lord, they would have recognised themselves. Whoever knows himself, knows his Lord. Whoever is ignorant of his Lord is ignorant of his self.

Whoever owns you will also be owned by you, and whomsoever you own must also own you.

The speech of the miser is bitter, even if it is true, and the speech of the generous one is sweet, even if it is false.

When you seek sensory things, meaning will seek you, and when you seek meaning, sensory things will seek you.

Dhikr has three stages. The first is *dhikr* of the outer without the inner and it leads to nothing. The second is *dhikr* of the outer and the inner, and it is sought after. The third is *dhikr* of the inner without the outer and it brings absorption, contemplation and witnessing.

Humility is a condition for the one who desires distinction. Whoever wants to be the master of his associates must first be the most humble of them. Humility for the seeker is like the walls of his house. Your reaching Allah is your reaching knowledge of Him. They say that your reaching Allah is your reaching a *wali* of Allah.

The Shaykh was asked when arrival would occur. He said arrival is that you do not seek arrival.

Speech only issues from men according to their station.

Remembering difficulties during times of ease is clarity.

Whoever seeks a way out of being a servant of Allah, is seeking something that Allah did not create.

The most intelligent person is he who wants to recognise himself by Allah. The most stupid person is he who wants to know Him by his self. The most knowing of people is he who wants to control himself by Allah. The most ignorant of people is he who wants to control Allah by himself.

Whoever is sincere in his quest benefits from the most ordinary people as he benefits from the most profound people.

The ugliest being is a mean Sufi. A true man of Allah is indeed generous. You pluck the fruit of what you plant.

The Prophet (S) said, "Show mercy to whoever is on the earth and whoever is in heaven will show mercy to you." When you are not generous, how can you seek generosity, and when you are not merciful, how can you seek mercy?

Knowledge of Allah is easy to obtain but understanding the creation of Allah is more difficult.

The use of (spiritual) power is to do with gatheredness, and the use of wisdom is to do with separation. The person of gatheredness says to a thing, "Be", and it is, by Oneness. The one of separation says to a thing, "Be", and it is, by duality. Use wisdom only with the common people and use power with the elite. As for the elite of the elite, they use them together, wisdom sometimes, and power at other times.

Whoever speaks a lot will make many errors.

One of the *'arifs* said, "They do not cross the valley of profit until they cross the valley of loss."

They say, "When you are with kings, watch your eyes. When you are with the people of outer knowledge, watch your tongue. When you are with the *'arifs*, watch your heart."

Sometimes wisdom emerges from the tongue of a scoundrel. Accept wisdom, even if it is from the mouth of a fool.

Those whom you confront with injustice will confront you with justice, and whomever you confront with justice, will confront you with injustice. That pertains to you and to existence. Such is the creation of Allah.

Speech is heavenly, and action is earthly. Gatheredness rules over separation and separation emanates from gatheredness. Whoever wants something must have its opposite.

Ibn Mashish says, "O Allah, some people ask You for domination over creation. I take refuge with You from that. I ask You to put me in such a position that I have no refuge or shelter, except You." The Prophet (S) says, "I am commanded to judge by the outer, for Allah alone knows the inner secrets." Distinction among creation is based on *zuhud*, which brings about might in the inner.

Whoever has a sound relationship with *Haqiqa* and realises there is no separation between it and him is the one who has mastery over this world and the next, and he is the *khalifa* of Allah.

Divestment is an ocean with no shore and contains both inwardness and outwardness. Its inwardness is *haqq* and he who persists in it will obtain its fruit by having power over heavenly and earthly things.

Blossoms are bitter, and their fruits are sweet. Meaning has sweet blossoms and bitter fruits. The blessed Prophet (S) said, "The garden is encircled by hated things and the fire is encircled by desired things." Divestment is gatheredness and meaning is separation. That is why it is said, "Connect your gatheredness and cut off your separation."

Allah has created knowledge and ignorance. By knowledge of Him, sovereignty exists, and by ignorance of Him, slavery exists. According to knowledge, freedom is great. The reality of knowledge is beauty and the reality of ignorance is majesty. Everyone's *himma* is according to their knowledge.

Information indicates absence from the object of information, because action cancels out words just as words cancel out action. Speech is by tongue and indicates a lack of witnessing. Witnessing invalidates information. The beginner seeks information from those who have arrived and are in the fields of witnessing. Knowledge of Allah relates to reaching Him and it is the knowledge of the people of witnessing.

The reality of poverty is annihilation in Allah and richness in Him.

Mirrors

Know that existence is a mirror for you and will reflect that with which you confront it. This applies to all of existence. This reflection is stronger for humans than it is for inanimate objects and plants. If you confront the son of Adam with good *adab*, he confronts you with good *adab*, and if you confront him with bad *adab*, he confronts you with bad *adab*. If you confront him with confusion, he confronts you with the same. If you confront him with humility, he confronts you with the same.

The right of he who looks at a person's wrong is wrong and the wrong of he who looks at person's right is right. Whoever sees people, sometimes rightly and sometimes wrongly, is sometimes right and sometimes wrong.

That is because existence is the mirror of yourself and you are the mirror of existence. Your attributes appear to you in the mirror of existence in the same way as the attributes of existence appear to you in your mirror.

When you confront existence with essence in the outer, it confronts you with attributes.

The mirror of existence is opposite the mirror of man. Whatever is in one mirror shines in the other one. When you confront existence with attributes in the outer, existence confronts you with its opposite, which is essence.

Existence confronts your majesty with beauty and the reverse is true. When your outer is beauty with creation, your inner is majesty with your self.

Divine power is like a mirror. You do not confront it with anything, but it confronts you with the same thing.

Transcendence

Transformation

Birds are of two types, those of the sensory world and those of the world of meaning. Nets catch sensory birds and the birds of meaning are caught by withdrawal and reflection. Sensory arrows shoot the birds of the sensory world and the arrows of meaning shoot the birds of the world of meaning. Their wings make the sensory birds swift in the outer world, and the birds of meaning make their homes in the spiritual heavens.

True withdrawal is giving up the company of fools and seeking the company of the wise and sincere. Withdrawal of the heart is for the strong seeker, and withdrawal of the form is to escape enslavement to this world. Withdrawal of the heart from form can lead to openings but can also be a barrier to real spiritual openings.

Transformation reflects both the outer and the inner and transformation in the outer is accompanied by transformation in the inner. The station of transformation along the path relates to outer transformation and corresponds to inner ongoingness.

Outer and inner transformation, or ongoingness, are like the seasons of winter and summer.

When essence manifests itself in man's outer, it moves him to his inner, and when the manifestation of attributes takes place in the outer, it moves him to the outer.

He who speaks about transformation is usually not amongst its people. He is simply among the ordinary people, though he desires transformation.

Discussion of love is a sign of love but does not necessarily signal arrival. Love is only longing, not actual arrival.

He who is annihilated by the Essence is the one who goes on by the attributes and is truly annihilated in Allah.

He who has going-on by the Essence is transformed by the attributes and has going-on in Allah.

The station of realisation relates to its foundation, which is ongoingness.

The first stage of transformation is from your humanity and the second is from transformation to a new transformation. Similarly, the first stage of ongoingness is going-on after transformation and the second is from going-on to ongoingness. Transformation relates to different stages of attributes and Essence.

Going-on in ongoingness is the source of the transformation of transformation and at the end of the journey is your Lord, and He says, "Oh, people of Madina you have no stopping place."

Transformation is humility and is death, whereas going-on is might and life, and the two join in man. If his transformation is in his outer, then his going-on is in his inner. If his going-on is in his inner, then his transformation is in his outer. His transformation is like death. Death is a door to the Garden and transformation is an entry to the Garden of Witnessing. One that is dead is not angry or joyful with anything.

The transformed one does not manage anything or choose anything, and all people are the same to him, poor or rich, friend or enemy.

The transformed one drowns in the source of Oneness.

Abdul Salaam Ibn Mashish says, "Drown me in the source of the sea of Oneness until I see, hear, find and feel only by It."

Diving into transformation veils you from going-on and the reverse is true.

The one with the station of going-on joins the presence of Allah and the presence of creation and gives everything its due. He is in the interspace between the two seas of *Shari'a* and *Haqiqa*, and these two seas are equal for him.

When man is transformed from seeing creation and only sees Allah in it, the humility that arises from this is the source of might. His poverty is the source of wealth. His weakness is the source of strength. His action in creation is by Allah, for Allah and to Allah. He does not see other than Him and he only sees the true King. On the other hand, when man is submerged in his veils and sees creation, it overcomes him, and he cannot distinguish between gatheredness and separation. This abasement is the most despicable and his poverty is the worst poverty.

He who acts by himself is deluded in every case. He occupies himself with his self and is a servant owned by his self. Allah has created the self for you as a servant and He bestowed it on you as a mark of honour. He gave it to you so that you might seek His help by it and serve Him in order to know Him. However, instead of becoming your Master's servant, you have become a servant of yourself and are heedless. The Qur'an reveals, "O man, your noble Lord did not deceive you. He created you, formed you, and shaped you." Allah says through the voice of the Prophet (S), "My servant, I created things for your sake and I created you for

My sake. Do not be diverted from what is yours to what you belong to."

Transformation has two aspects. The first is the transformation of existence by force and that is the transformation of the common people. The second is the transformation by choice and that belongs to the elite. Existence transforms the common people by force, which swallows them up. As for the elite of the elite, they transform existence and swallow it up inside them. Existence is your opposite and you are its opposite. Either Allah transforms you, or it transforms you by your choosing it. The difference between the common people and the elite is that the latter are the servants of Allah and possess existence by Allah while the common people are the reverse. They are the servants of existence and existence owns them. Ibn al-Farid says, "You are slain by what you love."

Arrival

Your eye can never be cool and tranquil unless you see through the light of *Haqiqa*. It is only then that it is at peace.

Shaykh Abdul Qadir al-Jilani said, "Your self contains all Reality. I use serious words and I do not deceive. There is nothing like this profitable knowledge. Enjoy it and recognise its truth. You are a *Haqiqa* by your own right."

Arrival is of two divisions: arrival of knowledge and arrival of ignorance. Ignorance belongs to the common people, for Allah says, "I am closer to you than your jugular vein." Knowledge belongs to the elite, and Allah says, "Are they the same, those who know and those who do not know?" Arrival of knowledge relates to reaching Allah by acquiring knowledge of Him. The light of majesty overcomes the ignorant and the light of beauty overcomes the one with knowledge.

Knowledge alone recognises ignorance and ignorance recognises knowledge. The ignorant is ignorant of himself, and ignorant of his ignorance of it, and the one with knowledge knows himself and knows his knowledge of it.

Higher manifestations relate to the world of the sensory and its meaning. They are called *waridat* and they alternate upon man like the water of the river. The water that flows in the river does not return and yet is never exhausted. It is foolish to try to contain a strong river. Allah has created the world so that you reach Him by it, while you are travelling or while you are at home.

Wealth is like a lion. Whoever meets it is startled and amazed, except the people of Allah, who are not concerned with existence or non-existence.

When the Great Creator gives a *tajalli* to someone, such a manifestation is immense. Things in creation become small for the recipient of the *tajalli*. Everything vanishes into dust and only *Haqq* (truth) remains.

The root of all progress is by sitting with the existential beings. By the knowledge you acquire from them, you acquire exaltation. When you acquire establishment by friendship, you acquire friendship with Allah and then you know His command of "Be and it is."

The sea of light, which separates the illuminated seeker from his Lord, destroys whoever enters it without a guide. Whoever finds the doorkeeper will reach Allah.

Nearness to Allah is to be far from the creation of Allah and to be near to the creation of Allah is to be far from Allah.

The enlightened one recognises his Master in all states for whatever appears to him veils all states. It is Allah Who manifests states and their opposites. He appears so He is not hidden, and He is hidden so He does not appear.

Whoever recognises Allah and unifies Him, only recognises Him and unifies Him regarding himself and his wealth. Whoever is ignorant of Allah and denies Him, he denies Him regarding himself and his wealth. The place of perfect profit is the place of perfect loss.

The Shaykh said that we only attain arrival by the earnestness of struggle like bees, struggling whilst they are gathered to Allah. Bees do not envy their brothers in work and thus they produce honey.

Fana' and *Baqa'*

The ordinary people respect the people of transformation because their station is high and elevated in the inner. Therefore, creation rejects them in the outer. The people of ongoingness are at the station of humility and weakness; therefore, the ordinary people accept them and seek them. Every seeker who has experienced transformation is travelling towards the station of ongoingness. Whoever has claimed going-on before transformation is deceived. When he who is in the station of ongoingness humbles himself to existence, all of existence humbles itself to him. He has majesty for himself and beauty for existence. It is the reverse for him who is still going on from transformation and has not reached the station of ongoingness after transformation.

Allah has created death in two aspects: sensory death and death of meaning. Sensory death implies removal of all outer obligations. Similarly, the death of meaning removes all inner obligations. In this way real intoxication with the Divine will veil all obligations. When a Shaykh was informed that someone had died, he stated that the obligation of formal prayers was now removed from the deceased.

For the people of the path, death relates to everything in existence which is transient and not real.

Enlightenment (Gnosis/*'irfan*)

'Irfan is knowledge of the way. It is not the way itself. Action is the way itself. *Himma* is the root of action and its branches.

When you see a man of Allah and he wants to take something away from you, know that he wants to give you something greater because real gain will follow.

The perfect *'arif* is always in the company of his Master and goes between separation and gatheredness. His separation is like the blink of an eye and his gatheredness does not veil him from his separation. His transformation does not veil him from his continuity and his continuity does not veil him from his transformation.

My Shaykh instructed me, "Do not be a lover of anyone (or anything), only the Beloved. If it is unavoidable, then only love the one who loves you."

My Shaykh's instruction to me was, "Only give wisdom to the one who needs it desperately. Otherwise, hide and hold back, for Allah says, '*Sadaqa* (charity, giving alms) is only for the poor and the wretched'."

The Shaykh has said to me, "Beware of discomforts! Beware of discomforts! Beware of discomforts in respect to yourself and in respect to others. If it besets you and discomfort is inevitable, then turn from it and recline on your back and rest from it, because discomfort is a burden. When two matters are forced upon one, the Shaykh chooses the easier of them."

The Shaykh said to me, "My son, by coming to me, whether you find me or not, you fulfil your need when you persist. That is what is required from you, and the goal is Allah, Who says, 'Whoever draws near Me by the span of a hand, I draw near him by an arm's length'."

My Shaykh counselled me saying, "Beware of being greedy. By 'greedy' I mean greed for leadership and greed for the heart. The last of what leaves the heart of an *'arif* of Allah is love of leadership and love of rank."

The Shaykh's advice was that, "There is nothing that I had come to do except join the two opposites and they obeyed me. If you perform an action, complete both it and its opposite, because no two things are joined without the permission of Allah."

GLOSSARY

A

Adab – courtesy, appropriate conduct

'Arif – gnostic, knower of God; possessor of *ma'rifa*

B

Baqa' – going-on in God, the mystic state once *fana'* has taken place

Baraka – blessing, grace

D

Dajjal – deceiver, imposter; an entity that causes confusion and chaos.

Dhikr/dhikru'llah – invocation, remembrance of Allah

Din – life transaction between Allah and man, religion.

Du'a' – supplication of Allah/God

F

Fana' – annihilation of the self/ego

Faqir – (pl. *fuqara'*) literally poor, impoverished, in need of Allah, implying pupils of a spiritual master

H

Hadith – tradition or report narrating the deeds or utterances of the Prophet Muhammad (S) but sometimes narrated by the Holy Imams of his family and Companions

Hadith qudsi – tradition or report in which Allah speaks in the first person through the tongue of the Prophet Muhammad (S).

Hammam – steam bath

Haqiqa – inner, ultimate reality, truth, science of the inner. From *haqqa* to be true, right, just, authentic, valid, and *haqqaqa* to realise, make something some true; the Divine Name, *al-Haqq*, the Truth, He whose being never changes

Hikma – wisdom. *Hikam*, a plural form, is also the title of the Shadhili Shaykh Ibn 'Ata' Allah's celebrated work.

Himma – spiritual yearning, an inner driving force.

I

'Ibada – worship, adoration.

Ihsan – performance and state of excellence, beneficence; the state of knowing that you are seen by Reality.

Ijtihad – an exercise of reasoning to establish the ruling of the *Shari'a* on a given point by a *mujtahid*, a person qualified for the enquiry.

Iman – faith, trust, belief, acceptance.

'Irfan – enlightenment, gnosis, inner knowing (verbal noun); *ma'rifa*, from the same root: inner knowledge, recognition of Reality.

I'tikaf – temporary retreat, usually in a mosque

J

Jinn – creatures made out of fire who exist in a parallel universe to humankind (ins), by contrast made out of clay.

K

Karama (pl. *karamat*) – miracles. That is events in the phenomenal world that implies a break in the causal chain.

Kafir – denier of Reality.

Khalifa – successor, representative, steward, to act on behalf of. Allah made Adam His steward on earth.

Khayal – subjective faculty of imagination by which we render shape, form and solidity into objective phenomena.

Khidhr – the servant of Allah with divinely inspired knowledge. The story of his interaction with the Prophet Musa (S) is narrated in the Qur'an (18:65-82).

M

Majdhub – ecstatic; god-intoxicated.

Malakut – realm of the spiritual, hidden, unseen world; between the realms of *Mulk* and *Jabarut*.

Miskin (pl. *masakin*) – destitute or indigent person.

Mu'min (pl. *mu'minun*) – believer.

Murid – pupil of a shaykh of instruction in Sufism.

N

Nafs – the lower self, ego

R

Rijal (pl. of *rajul*) – spiritual maturity, the man of Allah, Lit. man.

Ruh (pl. *arwah*) – The spirit, soul.

S

Sadaqa – charity, giving alms.

Shari'a – Islamic law or conduct, outward path, literally the path, the main road. *Shari'a* is the riverside from where one takes water.

Shaytan – Satan, the Devil; that force which leads you off the path.

Shirk – ascribing partnership to Allah, thus disaffirming Unity (*tawhid*).

Sunna – customary practice, line of conduct used in reference to Allah or the Prophet Muhammad (S).

T

Tajalli (pl. *tajalliyat*) – divine manifestation, witnessed by the inner eye of the seeker, theophany

Tariqa – lit. the path, the way, mystical school of guidance for those following the Sufi way.

Tawba – repentance, turning away from wrong actions.

Tawhid – Divine Unity, belief in Allah's Oneness.

U

Ulama – (sing. *'alim*) learned men/people of outer knowledge (knowledge of the *Shari'a*).

W

Wali (pl. *awliya'*) – lit. 'friend' of Allah. A reflection of the Perfect Man. See *wilaya*.

Waridat – inspirations, higher manifestations of meaning.

Wilaya – the station of gnosis; the authority of this station.

Z

Zahid – he who does without; continent from desires.

Zuhud – doing without; a precept of the Sufi path.

Glossary of Names Mentioned in the Extracts

Adam (Pbuh) – the father of all mankind.

'Ali Ibn Abi Talib, Imam, b. Makka, now in Saudi Arabia, d. Kufa, Iraq (d.40 AH, 599/600-661 CE) was the first Shi'ite Imam and the fourth of the Rightly Guided Caliphs (656–661 CE). He was the cousin of the Prophet Muhammad, the husband of his daughter, Fatima and the father of Imam Hassan and Imam Hussain, the second and third of the Shi'ite Imams. He was a pivotal figure in the development of early Islam and 'Nahj al-Balagha', the collection of his writings is greatly revered.

Al-Jilani, Abdul Qadir, b. Jilan, Persia, d. Baghdad, Iraq (470-561 AH, 1078-1166 CE). He was a celebrated theologian of the Hanbali School, jurist and mystic, who gave his name to the Qadiri Sufi order.

Al-Junayd, Imam, b. Baghdad, Iraq, d. Baghdad, Iraq (830-910 CE) was a key figure in the development of Sufi thought. His teaching circle in Baghdad was celebrated for its outer sobriety and adherence to *Shari'a*, whilst privately experiencing ecstatic states.

Al-Shadhili, Abul-Hassan, b. near Tangiers, Morocco, d. Humaithara, Egypt (593-656 AH, 1196-1258 CE). He was the pupil of Abd as-Salam ibn Mashish and the founder of the influential Shadhili Sufi Order.

Al-Shafi'i, Muhammad ibn Idris, Imam, b. Gaza, Palestine, d. Old Cairo, Egypt (150-204 AH, 767-820 CE), was the founder of the Shafi'i School of Islamic Jurisprudence. He travelled extensively in the Islamic world, spending years studying in Makka and Madina, before settling in Cairo. He was a student of Imam Ja'far al-Sadiq and Imam Malik ibn Anas.

Bistami, Bayazid, b. Bistam, Persia, d.Bistam, Persia (188-260 AH, 804-874 CE), one of the most influential early Sufi Masters, known for his ecstatic states.

Darqawi, Moulay al-Arabi al-, (1150-1239 AH, 1737-1823 CE), Moroccan Sufi Master, founder of the Darqawi Order, a revivalist branch of the Shadhili order. He was the pupil of Sidi 'Ali al-Jamal, a teacher of many awliya' in the Shadhiliyya, and responsible for collating his writings, extracts from which form this book.

Ibn 'Ashir, b. Fes, Morocco, d. Morocco (990-1042 AH, 1582-1631 CE) was a Maliki jurist and author of 'Matn Ibn 'Ashir', a textbook for the teaching of Islam in North Africa.

Ibrahim, Prophet (Pbuh) – Abraham.

Ibn al-Farid, b. Cairo, Egypt, d.Cairo, Egypt (577-632 AH, 1181-1234CE), a gifted mystic poet, known as the 'Sultan of the Lovers'.

Ibn 'Ata' Allah al-Iskandari, b. Alexandria, Egypt, d. Cairo Egypt (658-709 AH, 1259-1310 CE), Egyptian Maliki jurist and third Shaykh of the Shadhili Sufi Order. His writings, particularly the 'Hikam', 'Lata'if al-Minan' and 'Miftah al-Falah' formed an important part of the Shadhili teachings.

Ibn Mashish, Abdul Salam, b. Banu Arrus, Morocco, d. Jabal Alam, Morocco (d. 625 AH, 1228 CE), a reclusive Berber Sufi Master, who was the teacher of Shaykh Abul-Hassan al-Shadhili. He was the author of 'al-Salat al-Mashishiyya', a well-known prayer.

Jibril – the Archangel Gabriel.

Malik ibn Anas, Imam b. near Madina, Saudi Arabia and d. Madina (93-179 AH), was the originator of the Maliki school of jurisprudence, one of the four major schools of law in Sunni Islam. Shari'a based on Maliki doctrine is primarily found in North Africa, West Africa and the Gulf States. Sidi 'Ali Al-Jamal would have followed Maliki law.

Mursi, Ahmad Abul-Abbas, al-, b. Murcia, Spain, d. Alexandria, Egypt (616-686 AH, 1219-1287 CE). He was a pupil of Shaykh Abul-Hassan al-Shadhili, the founder of the Shadhili Sufi Order and is considered to his spiritual successor.

Musa, Prophet (Pbuh) - Moses.

Biographic Note about the Author

Sidi 'Ali ibn 'Abd al-Rahman al-'Umrani 'al-Jamal' (1090-1194 AH, 1675-1779 CE) was a great 'arif from Fes who lived to be over a hundred (either reaching 104 or 105). He earned the kunya (honorific teknonym) 'al-Jamal' (the camel) from the exclamations made by onlookers who saw him lifting a camel from the middle of the road and placing it to the side: 'He is indeed the camel!' Hagiography adds, in a play on this name, that he was known by the angels of Allah as al-Jamal (Divine Beauty).

During his long life, he served the Moroccan government administration before travelling to Tunisia where he learnt from the Sufi masters there. He later returned to Morocco to study further under other masters, among them the most notable being Sidi al-'Arabi ibn Ahmad ibn 'Abdullah al-Andalusi, with whom he remained for 16 years. After his passing al-Jamal built his zawiya in Fes.

He was the teacher of Moulay Muhammad al-Arabi al-Darqawi (d. 1823 CE), and it was from him that the Shadhiliyya–Darqawiyya takes its name. Moulay al-Darqawi's devotion to his teacher is reflected in his book The Darqawi Way, which contains many of Sidi 'Ali al-Jamal's teachings.

It is recounted in sources that Sidi 'Ali al-Jamal was greatly absorbed by witnessing the Prophet Muhammad, in both the sensory and the meaning, while asleep and also while awake:

> When a thought of the Messenger of Allah (S) would come to my mind, I would find him and his ten noble and righteous companions present before me, in the sensory and not just in the meaning, and we would speak with them and take

knowledge and works from the source of all knowledge and works.

In spite of his intense spiritual station and accomplishment in Islamic and Sufic sciences, he also engaged in trade, earning a reputation for astuteness. Sidi ʿAli was recognised by his successors to have been an axial shaykh (qutb) and support (ghawth) of his time.

Shrine and Zawiya of Shaykh Ali al-Jamal in Fes
taken from
https://fezgardenofthesaints.wordpress.com/2013/07/27/sidi-ali-al-jamal/

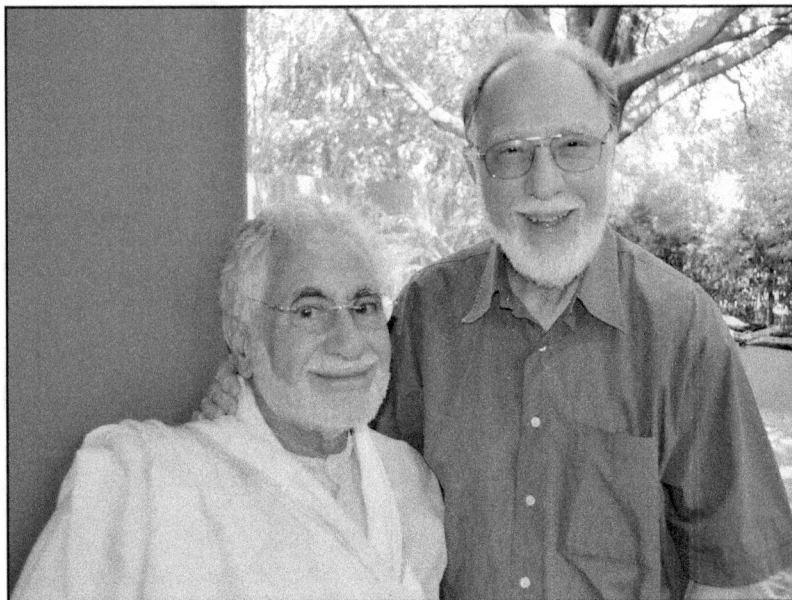

Selected and Translated by Shaykh Fadhlalla Haeri
and Shaykh Hosam Raouf

Shaykh Fadhlalla Haeri

Shaykh Fadhlalla Haeri is the author of many acclaimed books on Islam, the Qur'an and Sufism. From early on in his life he sought knowledge about the nature of existence, Reality and Truth. Much guidance and indications in this quest came to him through Qur'an and the Sufi paths.

Having felt a special affinity with the teachings of Sidi 'Ali al-Jamal, as well as those of other Shadhili/Darqawi Masters, Shaykh Fadhlalla Haeri wanted to share their insights with sincere seekers.

Shaykh Hosam Raouf

Born in Baghdad in 1934, Shaykh Hosam Raouf studied electrical engineering in the U.K. then worked in the oil industry in Iraq and later as a consultant in the UAE. His abiding interest in the religious and spiritual heritage of Islam and a natural orientation towards Sufism led him to delve deeper into the path to higher consciousness. A long-lived friendship with Shaykh Fadhlalla Haeri has led to many collaborations in teaching and research. He lives in Wales with his family.